A.FUNNY.THING.HAPPENED

Life behind the scenes - Hollywood Hilarity and Manhattan Mayhem!

By Lester Colodny with Susan Heller

Edited by Nikki Andrews

SciArt Media
Where science meets art...

Published by SciArt Media
www.SciArtMedia.com

A Funny Thing Happened Copyright © 2010 by Lester Colodny

Front and back cover designs Copyright © 2010 by SciArt Media

Inside photos are Copyright © 2010 by Lester Colodny or their respective copyright holders. All images used are from the personal collection of Lester Colodny, and are believed to be in the control of the author, or are used under fair use exemptions for educational purposes and/or parody.

All stories, content, and text are wholly the work of the author and do not necessarily reflect the views of SciArt Media.

Front and back cover design by James Maynard.

1st edition, first printed July, 2010.

No portion of this book may be reproduced, distributed or adopted for any purpose without the express written consent of the copyright holder(s).

A.FUNNY.THING.HAPPENED

Life behind the scenes - Hollywood Hilarity and Manhattan Mayhem

*To Paula
with love
Ruth Cobern*

Reviews of *A Funny Thing Happened*

"I've been a pal of Lester's since just prior to the invention of the wheel, so I can bear eyewitness testimony as to the veracity of many of the events he recounts in his book. And what a joy it has been to relive them through his hilarious pages! But there's great depth here as well. Since the very inception of show business both laughter and tragedy, side by side, have been its symbol. And under the surface of every side-splitting tale Lester tells is that ever present poignant layer of sadness. It's a hell of a read! And when Hollywood makes a movie of this book, I suggest they cast Lester Colodny as his own worst enemy!"
Marty Brill, *The New Dick Van Dyke Show*, *All in the Family*, *Three's Company*

"What's more fun than a barrel full of monkeys? Read Lester Colodny's *A Funny Thing Happened*, and you'll start finding out from the very first chapter. Along the way, you'll get to know some of the brightest stars in the comedy heavens, including the author himself."
Richard Lederer, former NPR host and author of *Anguished English*

"What fun! *A Funny Thing Happened* delivers laughs in every chapter and smiles to spare. Thank you, Lester, for preserving these hilarious stories. My only disappointment was when there was no more to read!"
Josh Judge, author, *Weather Facts and Fun* and *Extreme New England Weather*

"Any page that elicits laughter makes the book a comic treasure. While this review cannot expose every page of Lester Colodny's *A Funny Thing Happened*…it can assay a few, enough to justify pointing out this book as precious."

Richard Goldhurst, author, *Many are the Hearts: The Agony and the Triumph of Ulysses S. Grant.* Reader's Digest Press.

Table of Contents

The Today Show - 1957	1
In the Navy - 1943	11
Leonard - 1949	16
When I was a Youngman	21
The William Morris Agency - 1950	24
Come Up and See Me Sometime - 1951	28
The Belle of the Ball - 1951	32
The Tamiment and the Rowboat	38
Mel Brooks, Gofer. - 1953	42
A Really Big Shoo	52
The Martian Dialogue	59
Howie's Party - 1952	61
Living with the Stars	66
The Anti-Gravity Machine - 1960	70
Going to California 1956-57	74
After Dinner Mintz	86
A Sellers Market	93
How I Learned to Start Worrying and Hate Options	96
Two Bachelors and Six Kids	103
Roy and Irving	106
The Beatles are Coming - 1964	113
Life with Danny Simon	116
The Blind Date	119

The Baja Marimba Band	125
The Emmy Award	128
The Night Belongs to Charlie	130
Have Gene, Will Travel	137
Hugh and the Bunnies	143
Joan City	148
A Walk in the Park	156
The Universal Dream	160
The Cary Grant Story	171
Sidney's Secret	174
The Odd Brothers	187
A Munster Idea	193
Advertising Copy, Copy, Copy - 1969	201
Xerox	206
Sheriff Liz	209
Bulgaria is Just East of the Iron Curtain	213
Can you Wynn in Vegas?	216
An Offer Frank Couldn't Refuse	233
Leaving the Golden Land	242
The City, His City	248
The King and the Champion - 1986	251
Who the Hell is Arnie Frick?	266
How Much Would that Weigh?	270
On Televsion	272
A Minnow in a Shark Tank	276

Touchas on Tisch	278
The King's Ball	283
The Other Barbara	290
The King Calls	293
Hail Mary	299
After All That	306

Foreword by Elizabeth Hendrickson

Actress, *The Young and the Restless*, *All My Children*

Ever since I can remember, my Poppy, who you will soon be introduced to as Lester, was a story teller. Well, I guess that's what grandfathers do: prop their grandchildren on their laps and tell them tales of the unknown.

At a young age I sought to be a performer and all of his show biz stories were what I had him tell me over and over again. If it weren't for him I wouldn't be living my dream today as a professional actress.

Story teller aside, my Poppy was and continues to be an inspiration in my life. A man of many crafts and talents, he still continues to live his dream at eighty-four years of age. He is a constant reminder to never stop loving and living life, no matter what comes your way.

In this book I know that you will fall in love with his wit and charm, and you'll enjoy all of his stories just as he has told them to me all of these years. Unfortunately for you, you will not be propped up on his lap and see all of his funny little faces and hear him giggle as he relives what "happened." And if you don't like it then I'm going to go out on a limb and say that you're a nincompoop, just as my Pops would say it.

This book is in the vein of an oral history, a retelling of stories I have told through the years, and undertaken with story tellers' traditional liberties.

When I wrote this book I didn't think of it as fiction.

Lester Colodny is a very real person. And since I've drawn on my imagination to fill in details that are hazy (after all I'm eighty four) and I've changed some of the names to protect people's privacy, the only honest thing to do is call the book a novel.

Eternal thanks to my publisher James Maynard and my editor Nikki Andrews, without whose cooperation and continued enthusiasm this book would never have seen the light of day.

And a word of thank you to my three lunch buddies, Richard Goldhurst, Bill Abbot and Ed Van Gelder who week after week and month after month encouraged me to finish.

- Lester Colodny

*This book is dedicated to my wonderful wife Liz
and my marvelous sister Della.*

The Today Show - 1959

The Today Show, a live two-hour television program, was broadcast from seven to nine in the morning, five days a week. It starred Dave Garroway and featured news, politics, sports, fashion and the latest topics of the day. It had, as an associate producer and précis writer of the news—me.

Lester.

Lester Colodny. Five feet nine inches, one hundred seventy five pounds, dark curly hair. Twenty-nine years old, nice looking, good sense of humor.

Every morning, I would come in about four a.m. and read the news that came over the five teletype machines. Then I would digest what items I thought were timely, write a précis of them, and have the material ready for Frank Blair, our newscaster, to read on the air. Every other week, I met with our executive producer and the staff, and we planned out the rest of the shows. (The alternate weeks were prepared by another associate).

It was a grind but it was a job in television. And for a young guy like me, it was an adventure.

At the beginning of each of the two hours of the show, there was a five-minute period during which many of the various stations that carried the program were entitled to their local sponsors.

And one memorable morning when I had unexpectedly been put in charge of production, the star of the show, Dave Garroway, said to me, "You know, Chester, during the first five minute break, I was just thinking. What's funnier than a barrel of monkeys?"

I should have been warned. I should have realized that Mr. Dave Garroway was up to something. Especially when he called me Chester. But I was so involved with being totally in charge of everything that I overlooked Dave's well-known tendency to make mischief.

"You know the old expression, 'funnier than a barrel of monkeys?'" he asked.

"Yes?" I said warily.

"Let's find out. Get some monkeys, put them in a couple of barrels and when the show opens, we'll open the barrels and see what happens."

"You're not serious," I said.

"I'm dead serious. Go get me some monkeys."

"It's four a.m., Dave. Where am I going to find—?"

"That's what we pay you for," he said rather curtly, and walked away to talk to the newsman, Frank Blair, his associate Jack Lescoulie, and the woman of the month, the beautiful, talented and sweet Miss Florence Henderson.

It's not what they pay me for, I thought, but what the heck, the man wants monkeys, I'll find him monkeys.

I called the one place I knew that had monkeys: the Central Park Zoo.

"Hello. I'm with *The Today Show*. . . That's right. . . with Dave Garroway. You watch it every morning? Good. . . You love Dave? Good. . . He's real nice, good. Look, maybe you can help me. Is there anybody I could talk to about getting. . ."

The cast was assembled at the desk a minute before we went on the air and Dave asked me, "Where are my monkeys, Chester?"

Just then, two stagehands rushed in, pushing two dollies with three teetering barrels on them.

"Where do you want them?" one of the stagehands asked.

"Right in front of the desk," Dave directed.

The stage manager said, "Five, four, three, two, one," and signalled to Dave, who smiled into the camera.

"Hi there. Dave Garroway here. The twenty-third day of the month. I'm with my newscaster, Frank Blair, my really old pal, Jack Lescoulie, and the charming and very knowledgeable Miss Florence Henderson. We've been discussing with Chester Colodny, our producer, the old saying, 'What's funnier than a barrel of monkeys.' Well, we're going to find out. Ready, kids?"

"Ready," the three of them chimed.

"Ready, Chester?"

I held my breath.

The four performers leaned over the desk and pulled off the tops of the barrels.

Out leaped a bevy, a crowd, a horde, a multitude of monkeys, crazed from being penned up in barrels. Were they ever crazed!

One jumped on the table and started throwing pages of scripts around while another grabbed a cup of coffee and poured it over Frank Blair's head. A third started to pee on Jack Lescoulie's jacket and another masturbated on Dave. Two more fought on the desk for the right to hump Florence Henderson.

I stood there with the rest of the crew, frozen in horror, as the poor woman screamed and fended off her monkeys. The newsman yelled at the peeing primate and Dave swiped at them left and right.

Realizing that this was going over the air to several million viewers who were shaving, having their breakfast and (oh, no!) sending their children off to school, I ran to the control room.

The monitor screens, all fourteen of them, were filled with monkeys doing what crazed monkeys do—swinging from the lights, throwing scripts around, making balls of the papers on the desk, dipping them in spilled coffee and throwing them at one another. It was a mad, frantic scene.

The director was standing on his chair, yelling at his cameramen, "Go to four. . . no. . . three. . . no. . . no. . ."

I shouted, "Go to a commercial for Christ's sake. Go to black. Anything."

I looked around the studio.

The monkeys were up to more and wilder antics.

One was sitting on Jack Lescoulie, who was madly lashing out to get rid of him. Another had Dave Garroway's hairpiece in its mouth and was trying to eat it. Two of the monkeys were throwing the balls of coffee-dipped papers at Frank Blair, who was hiding under the desk.

I looked up at the monitors to see if the monkeys were still doing their things on network television. They were. Why didn't that stupid director go to black?

One of the monkeys swooped down from a microphone boom, rolled over on the desk and proceeded to fight the monkey who had a tight grip on Florence Henderson's breast. And they were getting it.

In spades and hearts.

And through it all, there were a dozen stagehands trying vainly to swat the moneys away with brooms and sticks.

As I ran back into the studio a woman stopped me.

"I'm looking for the producer," she shouted.

"That's me," I said.

"You'd better get your ass up to the twenty-ninth floor. Pronto. You're in a shitload of trouble."

A monkey swooped down from a light boom and swung onto the woman and kissed her. On the mouth.

Another monkey swung down and goosed her. She screamed.

I pulled the creatures off her and she ran down the hall and yelled, with an ear-piercing, "Twenty-nine! Go to floor twenty-nine!"

I turned to an assistant and screamed, "Get those frigging animals back in their barrels and get this place cleaned up. Pronto. I'll be right back."

I got out of the elevator on the twenty-ninth floor and crossed to one of the secretaries. "Someone wanted to see me?" I asked, trying to act nonchalant.

"Who're you?" she asked.

"The producer of *The Today Show*."

She said, "You'd better go right in."

I entered an office about the size of Madison Square Garden. At the far end, behind a massive desk, sat an elderly man. It was General Sarnoff, the president and chief stockholder of NBC. He was watching the Today show on ten different screens. He turned down the sound on the sets and beckoned to me.

"Sit," he said grimly.

I sat. On the edge of my chair.

"What's your name?"

"Lester Colodny."

"Are you the person who got those apes?"

"They're monkeys," I muttered.

"Apes, monkeys, what's the difference? Do you know who I am, Lester?"

"You're General Sarnoff," I said, and saluted.

"And you know what you just did?"

"I think so."

"You think so? You imbecile! You just featured a horde of apes—"

"They're monkeys, sir."

He ignored me.

". . .defecating, urinating and attempting to fornicate all over America's number one daytime television show!"

"That's pretty much how I see it, too," I said.

"Are you a producer? What's your job title?"

"I'm the associate producer and précis writer."

There was a pause. "What's a précis?"

"It's a—let's see. 'Dave Garroway ordered me to get barrels of monkeys. They defecated, urinated, and attempted to fornicate with Miss Florence Henderson.' That's a précis. Or, 'We fucked up,' which is an even more precise précis."

"I see. Well, I have a précis assignment for you. Go down to the studio and tell that arrogant, fat bastard Garroway that I am sick and tired of his adolescent antics and if he ever does anything like this again, I'll have him hung by the balls from the twenty-ninth floor. In fact, tell him I'll use piano wire."

"That's a little long for a précis, sir. It's more like a paragraph."

"Go."

"Yes sir."

I couldn't believe the president of the network had not fired me.

I would have canned me.

I would have fired my ass right out of that studio.

I would have made sure I never got another job in television for as long as I lived.

There wasn't a reason in the world not to fire the dunce who got conned into the stupidest stunt in history.

None whatsoever.

But instead of canning me he gave me a raise.

I walked into Dave's office.

Here I was, this upstart kid, about to tell a huge television star that his ass was in a sling. I was more than a little nervous. I was also furious.

"Dave—" I began.

He said, "Those monkeys weren't the greatest idea, were they, Chester?"

"No," I agreed. "Not the greatest."

"I thought they were a great idea," he sulked.

"What you thought and what happened were two very different things," I said.

"Did you know one of them tried to crap all over me?"

"I saw that," I said with a quiet smile.

"And did you see the faces of those two who were vying for Florence?" he asked.

"Everyone in America saw it, Dave."

"Don't tell me," he gasped.

"Yup. Every moment of the action. The General was watching, too."

"The General?" Dave asked morosely.

"Yes. And he had a few, shall we say, trenchant remarks that he wanted me to pass on to you."

"He did?"

"Yes."

"What did he say?" he asked in a choked voice.

I was feeling my oats. And I was still mad about being caught up in his dumb scheme. "He said that if you ever, ever, do anything even remotely like that again—" I paused for dramatic effect—"he would have you hung by your scrotal sac out the window of the twenty-ninth floor. He said not to forget to mention he would be using piano wire."

"Oh God," Dave moaned. "He said that?"

Before I could answer there was a knock at the door and it flew open to reveal one very angry, rumpled, bedraggled, but still stunningly beautiful Florence Henderson.

"I quit," she spat through clenched teeth.

"You, you can't do that," Dave sputtered.

"The hell I can't," she said. "You stupid, asinine jerks can take your frigging show and shove it up your rear ends."

She left.

"Did you hear that? Did you hear what she just said to me?" Dave exclaimed.

"Yes, sir, I did. Every word of it."

I met Mr. Sarnoff at a convention several months later. I said, "I beg your pardon, General, but do you remember me?"

"No," he said.

"Let me remind you. I'm Colodny, the producer/précis writer on *The Today Show*, with Dave Garroway. I'm the one who had the Central Park Zoo deliver monkeys to the set. Remember?"

"That was you?"

"Yes, sir."

He said to a man next to him, "Hey, Jim, remember the story I told you about the monkeys?"

"Oh, yeah. It was hysterical. You make up the craziest stories."

"Really?" said the General, turning to me. "Tell him."

I also ran into Florence Henderson, years later, when I was directing a commercial for Needham Harper and Steers Advertising. I had told the story of the monkeys countless times (at the urging of the senior creative director, Lois Korey, who thought it was a panic). We were producing a commercial for frozen grilled cheese sandwiches (frozen grilled cheese sandwiches?) and the spokeswoman was Florence Henderson.

When she saw me she ran across the room, threw her arms around me, and shouted, "Lester, you old son of a gun. I haven't seen you since that monkey tried to screw me."

"You mean, it's true?" asked Lois. "The story about the monkeys is true?"

Florence said, "True?" She pulled her pants leg up and showed us a scar on her right thigh.

"That's from monkey business," she said.

In the Navy - 1943

I went to college for a year. But the war was on so as soon as I could, I joined the navy.

Like so many others at that time, I was utterly unaware of what war was, what it meant. I was proud of my country and even prouder of myself in uniform.

I was only seventeen.

So I did some growing up in boot camp. And I pretty much figured the rest out as a seaman on an LCI (Landing Craft Infantry), which ferries soldiers and equipment from ships to the shore.

On my nineteenth birthday, our boat was carrying a load of soldiers from a troop transport to a place called Samar, off the coast of the Philippines.

That morning I went out on deck, and heard the captain say over the loudspeaker, "Attention all members of the crew. You will wear clean white hats for the invasion."

I'm telling you, you can't make this stuff up.

To say that the captain was an idiot would be a serious understatement. He was a waiter from Cleveland, and had no business being a maitre d' let alone heading up a troop transport boat.

So there we were, in clean white hats, while the soldiers, in full battle regalia, were praying because the beach was taking an enormous pounding from the enemy.

As we got about twenty yards from where we were going to drop our ramp into shallow water, the shelling increased in range and numbers.

The captain got hysterical.

"Get us off this beach. Now!" he screamed.

"We're not on the beach, Captain," someone yelled.

"Get us off this beach!" the captain shouted again.

We ignored him. We knew we had to get close enough to the beach so that our soldiers wouldn't drown when we dropped them off in the water.

The captain's voice was a shrill scream. "Are you going to get this fucking boat out of here?"

"Hold your fucking horses, Captain," I shouted. "You want these soldiers to drown?"

"I don't give a shit," the captain yelled. "Get us outta here."

The crew yelled in unison, "Fuck you, Captain!"

Then a shell hit our LCI. The boat fell over. Sideways.

And sank like a stone.

Fortunately, by that time we had gotten into water that was only five feet deep and the soldiers scrambled off safely. The crew followed.

Including me.

We were no dopes.

"Where the fuck are you going?" bellowed the captain.

I suppose we made a response but no one could hear it, what with the shells and shrapnel falling all around us.

It probably made "Fuck you, Captain" sound like "Silent Night."

I was scared witless.

When we hit the beach, I saw that the soldiers and sailors were digging holes in the sand and lying down in them to keep the shrapnel from hitting them, so I did the same.

I dug like a crazed dog to make a hole deep enough to leap in and bury myself. Then I covered my body with enough sand so that if an enemy bullet or shrapnel came my way, the chances were it wouldn't get to me.

At least I prayed it wouldn't.

I was never a great believer. In fact, I was kind of an agnostic. But like the old saw goes, you never heard such prayers going up to heaven in your life as you heard from that very shallow foxhole.

I lay there for what seemed like hours, with bombs and machine gun bullets spraying everywhere, and then, suddenly, it was quiet.

I waited.

Then I waited some more.

Finally, slowly, I raised my head enough to peer out of my hole.

There were men all along the beach, coming up out of their holes.

Thousands of soldiers and sailors and marines.

All along the beach.

I didn't know what to do. I didn't even have a rifle. I looked around to see if any of my boat mates had dug in nearby.

And then one of the most surreal moments of my life occurred.

I heard a voice say, "Aren't you Lester Colodny from Brooklyn College?"

I looked over at the next hole. Standing there was a tall skinny guy in an army uniform. The soldier's hair was matted from hiding in his helmet and his face was covered with sand. "You're Lester Colodny from Brooklyn College. I remember you!"

I gaped at him in disbelief.

"What ever happened to Shirley Kaminsky with the big tits?" he asked.

This wasn't happening. It couldn't be. I was thousands of miles from home, on a beach that was being shelled by an enemy I couldn't see, and this guy was asking me about Shirley Kaminsky's tits?

"What a piece she was," the soldier said.

I stood there and wondered if I was having a nightmare, a day-mare, a hallucination.

The soldier said, "She really had a pair of kumquats."

I was speechless. I stared at him in utter amazement.

He didn't seem to notice. "I ask you, did you ever, ever in your life see such a beautiful pair of jalabos?"

I didn't have a reply. I saw other men walking in one direction on the beach and turned around to do the same.

The soldier followed me.

I whirled around. "Jesus Christ, man, I don't know," I yelled. "And I don't care."

"I care," the soldier said. "That Shirley sure had a pair. . ."

Suddenly there was a huge sandstorm. It was like the blast from a tornado. The pressure wave threw me backwards and slammed me into the beach.

I shook my head to clear my eyes of sand.

The soldier from Brooklyn wasn't there anymore.

I walked down the beach with all those thousands of American soldiers and sailors and marines, and thought about Shirley Kaminsky.

He was right. She sure had a pair of jalabos.

Leonard - 1949

About this time, I met Leonard Grainger. He was a booking agent who worked the little clubs and hotels around New York. I found his address through a minuscule ad in Variety. It was in a small office, just off Broadway, with a desk, two chairs and a pay telephone on the wall.

(How the world has changed. How was I to know that meeting Leonard would alter my life completely?)

The first words he said to me were, "Close the door, there's a draft. Now, what can I do for you?"

"I'm a comic," I said.

"Any experience?"

"I destroyed the audiences in the Navy."

He frowned. "But no experience commercially?"

"No."

"You do impressions?" he asked.

"No, but I have real good material," I said.

"But no impersonations."

"No."

"Can't you imitate James Cagney?" he insisted. "Even my cousin Irving does Cagney. And he's a butcher."

"I'm sorry," I said and got ready to leave.

"Okay. Tell me a joke," he said.

"My mother was the worst cook. She burned water."

He smiled.

I continued, "My mother's idea of a gourmet meal was spaghetti with ketchup."

"That's not bad. The rest of your stuff is that funny?"

I nodded.

He opened his top drawer, took a nickel from a pile, dropped it into the pay phone and dialed.

"Hello," he said into the phone, "is Ziggie there?. . .Tell him Leonard Grainger is on the phone. . .the agent. . .Hello Ziggie? I found an emcee for you. . .I know. . .I know the last one I sent you stuttered . . .but this guy has real possibilities. He's a comer. Good. Okay. . .Fine . . .his name?"

Leonard looked at me.

"Lester Kay," I whispered.

"Lester Kay. . .what? Look, give him a shot. One night. If he doesn't work out, you don't have to pay him. . .Okay. . .sure. . .fine."

He hung up.

"You're booked into Ziggie's Playpen, Bronx, Hundred-Thirty-Fifth Street and Broadway, starting tonight at ten. If you last, you'll do five shows a night, six nights a week. A hundred fifty a week. Less commission."

"A hundred fifty less ten percent is a hundred thirty five. Thirty shows a week? That comes to about four dollars and fifty cents a show."

"You want it?" he asked.

"Yes," I said.

On my way out, he said, "My commission is fifteen percent."

It was dark in the vestibule of the club and a girl at the door insisted I pay fifty cents to get in. I tried to explain that I was going to be working there when a huge man came over.

"What's doon?"

"This guy won't pay the cover charge," whined the girl.

"You the emcee?" the big guy asked.

"Yes."

"Where the fuck you bin? You're a half hour late. You're on. Do a coupla minutes and introduce the first girl."

He handed me a slip of paper and I ran up to the middle of the room to a circular stage around which sat about four or five dozen men. They were clapping their hands in unison.

"Good evening, ladies and gentlemen."

I noticed that there were only men in the audience.

"You know, a funny thing happened to me on the way to Ziggie's Playpen—" I started.

I noticed that the bar was moving. Rotating actually. Going around in a circle. It was maddening.

I tried my best jokes. Nobody laughed. I tried some of Milton Berle's best jokes.

Still nothing. Then I stole one from Henny Youngman.

The audience just stared at me.

No one was listening because the stage was turning so some people heard the beginning of the joke, some people the middle, and some the punch line.

Giving up, I reached into my pocket.

"And now," I read, "Ziggie's Playpen presents," I glanced down at the paper, "the one, the only, Georgia peach, Miss Georgia Southern."

I heard a roar from the crowd. It was a small crowd and a big roar. They didn't give a damn whether I was bad or good. No one gave a shit about me. Georgia Southern was what they were waiting for.

From out of the darkness a stunning girl appeared, undulating to the music from a three piece band. She was a stripper.

I got off the stage and groped around in the darkness until I found a door, dimly lit, marked "dressing room." It was occupied by three other girls, each one of them more gorgeous than the others.

Now that I think about it, they were all half-naked. But I didn't notice. I was too depressed to notice.

"Hey kid," one of them said, "those were funny jokes."

"Nobody laughed," I protested.

"So what?"

"I'm the new emcee. I don't want to get fired before the second show. But I tell the first part of a joke to guys over here," I gestured to my front, "and by the time I get to the punch line, even if I rush, I'm telling it to the guys over there." I jerked my thumb behind me.

They looked at me and laughed.

"Listen kid," one of the girls said, "I been working here in this shithouse for three weeks now. Three weeks, six nights a week, five shows a night. That's ninety shows so far. And you wanna know somethin'? There are guys who come in here every night, for every show, and do you know, they've still never seen my tits."

I understood.

Later that night, I called Leonard.

I said, "I think you'd better find another comic for Ziggie's Playpen. One who does James Cagney and Edward G. Robinson. Maybe your cousin."

When I was a Youngman

I left Ziggie's an ex-comic but Leonard became my friend for life. Once we established that I was a dreadful comic but a good writer, Leonard and I became great friends and we got down to business. We had breakfast and lunch together and he looked for work for me.

One day he said, "Lester, you know Henny Youngman, don't you?"

(Henny Youngman, in case you don't know, was a stand-up comedian. One of the stars of the time.)

"Go over to Lindy's restaurant and ask for him. He's cheap, but he's always on the lookout for good jokes. Maybe you can sell him some."

I was standing outside of Lindy's (a famous watering hole where all the comics, singers and other entertainers in New York convened every night) when Henny Youngman came by.

As he was entering the restaurant, I said, "Excuse me, Mr. Youngman, can I talk to you for a second?"

"What is it?" he snapped.

"I'm Lester Colodny, I'm a writer—"

"So go write."

"I mean, I write jokes. Leonard Grainger told me that you might be in the market for—"

"Grainger? Yeah? Tell me a joke you wrote."

I said, "A pan handler came up to me and said, 'I haven't had a bite for days.' So I bit him."

"Not bad. Tell me another one."

"My wife is the worst cook. She burns water."

"Write me a bunch of jokes. And meet me here tomorrow."

"What time?"

"Same time."

I went back to Leonard's and told him, "I met Henny Youngman and told him two jokes. I think he liked them."

"Which jokes?"

"'I bit him' and 'my mother burns water.' I have an appointment with him tomorrow. Maybe he'll buy."

That night I wrote until dawn. And I was standing outside of Lindy's when Henny Youngman came by the following evening.

"Mr. Youngman?" I said.

"Yeah?"

"Remember me? Lester Colodny? Leonard Grainger sent me. I've got the jokes for you."

"Oh yeah, lemme see."

I handed him three pages of jokes. He read them all, took out a pen and marked off seven.

"I'll take this one, this one. . .these two. . .and these three. Type 'em up and send them to me." He handed me his card.

It read:

>Henny Youngman, Comedian
>Also Weddings & Bar Mitzvahs
>East 11th Street, New York, N.Y.
>Call 555-7894 or leave a message
>with the barber downstairs.

I was ecstatic.

As he turned to enter the restaurant, I said, "Excuse me, Mr. Youngman—"

"What is it?"

"How about, you know, paying for them?"

"For what?"

"The seven jokes."

"Oh yeah," Henny said.

He pulled up one of the sleeves of his sports jacket. There on his arm were about two dozen wrist-watches. He pulled off one with an elastic band and handed it to me.

I said, "What's this?"

He said, "That's a very valuable watch."

"A watch?" I said.

He said, "That watch is worth at least seven jokes."

I protested, "But Mr. Youngman, how do I pay my agent?"

He said, "Give him the band."

The William Morris Agency - 1950

I had teamed up with my friend Herby Reich and we started to get some writing work like television sketches for *Hellzapoppin*, continuity work for *The Eddie Cantor Show* and some comedy bits for *The Jerry Lester Show*.

Though we weren't making much money, we were starting to get a name for ourselves.

It was then that an agent from the William Morris Agency, one of the biggest in the business, asked us if we would like to be represented by them. I was so flattered.

Herby said he wanted a real job with regular paychecks, and went off to write manuals for some electronics firm.

I, on the other hand, said, "Sure, absolutely," and signed up.

For seven years.

This was it. The Big Time. I had officially arrived.

For the next three weeks I couldn't get my agent on the phone. I couldn't even get the receptionist to admit he worked there. I called and called. What the hell was going on?

I got so mad I decided to go to the Morris office in person.

It was full of hopefuls: writers, actors, singers, dancers, all camped out in the office in hope of being knighted with the honor of William Morris representation.

I told the receptionist I was there to see my agent. She told me to have a seat.

I sat among the untouchables, the artists who were not officially anybody, from whose ranks I had just been promoted three weeks earlier.

I couldn't see much difference between us.

Some of them asked how I got my agent, and I really didn't know how to answer them. Then they wanted to know how the process worked, what kind of jobs I'd gotten.

I still didn't have an answer.

After sitting there for forty-five minutes, I got up and went back to the receptionist. She told me that my agent wasn't in.

Wasn't in? What the hell was I doing sitting there waiting for him? "Can you tell me when he'll be in?"

"No."

"I don't understand," I said. "I'm a client of the office."

"I'm sorry," she said, with a blank look.

I snapped.

I looked around at all the unsigned talent and hollered, "This, this is how my agent does business? This is complete crap. If I couldn't be a better agent than him I'd hang up my jock."

I don't know why I said it and I didn't know what to do after I'd said it.

It was incredibly crude. I was embarrassed to death.

I was starting to slink toward the exit when a tiny little man came up to me. "What's your name, son?" he asked.

I told him.

"And you say you're a client of this office?"

"Yes."

"What do you do?"

"I'm a writer."

"What do you write?"

"Comedy."

"I heard what you just said," he replied.

I said, "I'm sorry. I was. . .so. . .so. . ."

"Frustrated?" he offered.

"Yes."

"Do you really think you could do a better job than your agent?" he asked.

"With one hand tied behind my back," I declared.

"Come with me," he said.

Now I realize, dear reader, you're thinking that this is way too pat. Not real life. But so help me, this is what happened.

I followed him through the double doors to a small office.

He said, "This is your office. You are now an agent with the William Morris Agency. You'll receive one hundred fifty dollars a week plus expenses. You'll be handling comedy writers." With that he left.

Just like that.

I later learned his name was Martin Jurow and he was one of the bosses at the William Morris Agency.

Now, I had mouthed off pretty good and to tell the truth, I didn't have any idea what the hell I had to do next.

So I sat down behind the desk and waited.

I didn't know what I was waiting for, but I guessed that sooner or later someone would come by and ask me what I was doing behind this desk and I could ask him, or her, what an agent for comedy writers did.

And sure enough, someone did.

Which explains how I found myself as an agent, with no experience of any kind, at the William Morris Agency.

Come Up and See Me Sometime - 1951

After being discharged from the United States Navy, I'd gone back to college and then to graduate school. There I authored, starred in, produced and directed several shows, some of them original musical comedies.

Those were heady days. In the early sixties a person, at least this person, did whatever came along. Especially if it was in show business. If anyone asked, I was a writer, an emcee, a comic, an actor. Name it. I was it.

One summer day I was strolling down Broadway when I happened to bump into Hilly Elkins. Hilly was only an office boy at a talent agency but he had discovered an important phenomenon. If he dressed in a Chesterfield coat (with a fur collar) and a homburg hat, people in the theatrical business would consider him to be a producer. It didn't matter how old he was or what experience he had, the coat and hat got him into backers' auditions.

And there it was, in bold letters, on the marquee of the Fifty-sixth Street Theater, on the Great White Way:

Hilly Elkins
In Association with the Theatre Guild
presents
MAE WEST
in
Diamond Lil
Three Weeks Only

How this twenty-one-year old had inveigled his way into co-producing this revival was beyond my ken. It was astonishing.

He asked me what I was doing and when I told him "nothing" he said, "Go in and tell the stage manager that I sent you. Miss West will be casting the show this afternoon. Maybe you'll get a role." Just like that.

Now, I was pretty sure of getting a part. I had played the lead in any number of college plays and I was pretty certain that I had the stuff to make the grade. Maybe not the lead opposite Mae West but surely a fairly major role.

What should I do for my audition? I thought. Shakespeare? Or maybe a Will Rogers monologue?

When I entered the theater that afternoon, the casting director had about four dozen men lined up around the stage waiting to audition.

My mind was a whirlwind. I didn't want to blow this opportunity, but I couldn't decide what material to do.

We stood there a while appraising one another. When was the director going to start letting us audition? There were an awful lot of us standing around.

Suddenly Mae West appeared. She was breathtaking. She was unbelievable. She was about sixty but she still had that outrageous demeanor that said provocatively, "Come up and see me sometime." Mae West, even now, had that incredible magic.

She slithered around the stage and slowly looked each one of the men over. Up and down.

She said to her secretary, in that sexy, lilting voice, "Him." The man stepped forward.

She eyed a few of the others and sashayed past them. Then, "Him." That man stepped forward and joined the first one.

She passed a few others. She reached out to check the biceps of the next guy. He flexed with all his heart and soul. She laughed that indescribable Mae West laugh and said, "And him." He practically jumped forward.

"Him. And him. And him." The three stepped forward.

And then she got to me.

I didn't know about anyone else, but I never felt so naked in my life, standing right there on the stage of the Broadway Theater. I felt like a hundred and fifty eight pounds of chopped sirloin.

"And. . .him," she said, pointing at me. I stepped forward.

That was the audition. No monologue, no acting, just "him."

Miss West disappeared. The stage manager handed each one of us "sides" (the roles we were to play with cues) and told me I was to play an escaped convict who was being hidden in Mae West's bedroom during the opening of the second act. There would be three rehearsals and a dress technical for the lights and sound, all without Miss West.

The play was based on one that Mae West had written in 1933 and made into a movie. It was all about a saloon singer in the 1890s who sets out to seduce a Salvation Army officer.

I never read the entire script (I never got the whole thing) but it didn't matter because the only thing the audiences came to see was Mae West.

So there we were, on opening night. The house was packed as Mae West, in full regalia, with an enormous boa around her neck, sashayed wonderfully down the curved stairway (built especially for her) singing the opening number.

It was absolutely mind-boggling.

No one gave a hoot whether the show was any good or not. They had all come to see this incredible performer.

The curtain came up on the second act and there I was, lying in the second level of the set, next to. . .Mae West.

Mae West and me. The sex legend and Lester Colodny.

And as she wriggled into place she whispered to me, "Hey kid, do I make you hot?"

I remember thinking, at that moment, of the line she had thrown at Cary Grant in the movie *She Done Him Wrong*: "Is that a gun in your pocket or are you just glad to see me?"

I want you to know, that was no gun in my pocket.

The Belle of the Ball - 1951

Not long after I was discharged from the Navy I met Edy at Brooklyn College. I thought about her for months, for years. She was a platinum blond, with long gorgeous legs, a terrific bosom, and a way about her that made men swoon.

She was the belle of the ball and just about everybody I knew was hot for her.

Including me.

I remember pursuing her with flowers, with candy, with beseeching pleas for her love. Day after day, night after night, I dreamed about touching her, fondling her, cuddling with her, holding her. Even. . . whatever. I was overcome. Crazed. Maddened. Everywhere I looked, I saw. . .Edy.

Now you may ask, and you have the right to ask, what was a nice fellow like me doing, falling for a girl like Edy? Well, I'll tell you. I wanted, I ached, I had to—you know.

I simply had to have her. And I got what I longed for. At twenty-two, I married Edy. She was mine.

On the first night of the honeymoon I lay in the tropical moonlight, holding my breath, waiting.

Then she appeared, backlit in a diaphanous gown, her long, exquisite legs outlined in a fantastic glow.

She approached the marriage bed, slipped off the gown and slithered into my arms. I was aroused to a fever pitch, but I restrained myself and slowly kissed her nose, her cheeks and her mouth.

She leaned toward me and put her lips to my ears and whispered. I shivered in delight.

And I heard her say, "Maralyn Cohen's tits are silicone."

Edy was the world's leading authority on everything. In fact, she was the leading authority on things that weren't invented yet. She was sexy, incredibly sexy, except that she never stopped talking.

So although I was, at the time, very much into sex, I rarely shared the same feelings at the same time that Edy did. It was frustrating, to say the very least.

When we went out with friends I'd hear male friends muttering behind my back to one another, "How would you like to get into that one?"

I'd like to have known how they would have done it. Get into her.

Because Edy was a flirt. An unconscionable, outrageous, impossibly flippant player of men's emotions.

She made eyes at doormen, tossed her long golden hair at policemen, wiggled her hips at Con Edison workers peeking out of their holes in the streets. She winked at salesmen at Bergdorf's, blew kisses to passengers on buses, and breathed heavily in the ears of friends, business partners and even strangers, when I was out of sight.

At first it was amusing. After a while, it became a pain, a really big pain, in the behind.

Bernard Seligman and Charlie Baker, two of my fellow agents at the William Morris office, knew that in my heart of hearts, I wanted to be an actor and writer. They were very sympathetic. Bernard used to sit with me and say, "What the hell are you doing here at the Morris office? You have so much talent. Why don't you audition for a show and do something with your life?"

I would sit and listen to him, nod, smile ruefully, then throw up my hands and go sell another writer or director. I was a hopeless case.

One day Bernard came into my office and closed the door.

"Lester," he said, "I just heard from Charlie Baker that they're casting for the London company of *Guys and Dolls*."

"So?" I said.

"So, we want you to audition."

"We?"

"Charlie and me."

"Get out of here," I said.

"No, really. This is your chance. You'd be perfect for *Guys and Dolls*."

"How am I going to audition even if I wanted to? They would recognize me in a second."

"No they won't. Abe Burrows, the director, is holding the auditions. He doesn't know you. And you'll go under another name. I already told Sid Bernstein, the assistant, all about you. He knows. He'll keep quiet. And you'll audition under the name Leo Cinder."

"You're not kidding me, are you?" I asked.

"For Chrissakes, Lester. Go. It's the chance of a lifetime."

"When?" I asked cautiously.

He said, "Next Monday. At noon. You can go on your lunch hour and no one will know the difference."

"I'll think about it," I said.

But I was already planning what I would do. I quickly learned the lyrics to "Sit Down You're Rockin' The Boat," read the script that Charlie had gotten for me, and was ready and tingling at noon on Monday.

I walked into the Forty-Eighth Street Theater on Monday at a quarter to twelve and my knees were knocking. Finally, I had a chance to really prove myself.

Sid Bernstein winked at me and called out, "Leo Cinder," and I strode out on the stage.

I nodded to the accompanist and sang. Fortunately for me, it was one of those golden moments, and I hit every note, every nuance, just right. I could feel it.

Then I read a few parts with Sid. There was silence in the theater.

Then a voice came out of the darkness. "Mister Cinder. Wouldjoo please come out to the apron?"

I walked to the edge of the proscenium and peered into the darkness. "Yes?" I said.

"What do you do? I mean, you're an actor?" the voice said.

"Yes." I answered uncertainly.

"Do you have a regular job?"

"As a matter of fact, yes." I answered. I was busted.

Shit.

"You're not a member. . .a part of. . .you're not connected with. . . the mob, are you?"

I was so happy I could have died on the spot. I had read the part of Big Julie so well that he thought I was. . .I was overcome.

"No, sir," I said. "I have a legitimate job."

There was a pause. I heard whispering. Then, "Mr. Cinder, how would you like to go to London, play a small part and understudy all the secondary parts of the show?"

He was offering me the opportunity I had always dreamed about. In a smash hit show.

I said, "Can I give you my answer tomorrow?"

"Tomorrow, yes. But no later."

I floated out of the Forty-Eighth Street stage entrance on a cloud of absolute bliss.

I jumped in a cab and went home. Edy was just getting ready to go out.

"Edy, sit down, I want to talk to you."

"What are you doing here in the middle of the afternoon?"

"That's what I want to talk to you about."

I told her about the audition and the offer to go to London.

She looked at me with a strange expression and said, "You're going to be an actor?"

"Yes. In *Guys and Dolls*."

"You've got a good job. You're doing really well at the agency. And you're going to go to London to be an understudy? Are you crazy? Why would you want to give that up to be a lowly assistant actor?"

"But Edy—" I protested.

"Lester, let's stop this nonsense. Besides, I have a meeting to go to." She left.

I turned down the offer. I don't know why. It was the culmination of a dream and I refused it.

In retrospect, it was probably a good idea. I wouldn't have my beautiful wife Liz, my six children and twelve gorgeous grandchildren today.

Though I can't help but wonder what might have been.

Tamiment and the Rowboat

About a year later, I got a job moonlighting at a summer theater. Instead of taking my two weeks of vacation, I worked at the agency from Monday to Thursday so I had Friday, Saturday and Sunday writing sketches and special material at the Tamiment Playhouse, in the Pocono Mountains. It was a breeding ground for would-be comedians, singers, dancers and writers. Every week, believe it or not, the resident company performed a new revue for the guests at Tamiment Lodge.

Every weekend, Edy and I would get into my old Packard convertible and drive to the Poconos where I would hand the troupe the sketches I had written at home in Greenwich Village, for the next week's shows. Edy came along to make snide remarks.

One Saturday afternoon, while the cast was rehearsing one of my sketches, I happened to look out the window of the casino attached to the Lodge and, lo and behold, there she was, out on the lake, in a rowboat, with a fellow who had a moustache.

Not that the moustache bothered me, exactly. But it seemed to me that it was not exactly fitting for a married woman to be rowing around the lake with a strange man, while I was inside rehearsing a sketch.

That Sunday night, as we were driving back to New York, I mentioned, "Wasn't that you in the rowboat with that fellow with the moustache?"

She said, "Yes. He was rowing the boat. I was riding."

I said, "Well, don't you think it is. . .how shall I say? Somewhat unseemly for you, a married woman, to be in a rowboat with someone with a moustache, especially since I don't even know the man?"

She said, "No. I don't think so."

At the time we were nearing the Lincoln Tunnel (it goes under the Hudson River from New Jersey to New York) and the traffic lines were interminable. We were creeping along at about three miles an hour when I said to her, "Well, don't you think that there's a chance that you were not acting like a good wife being in that rowboat with a man?"

(This time I didn't mention the moustache).

She said, "No. I don't think it was unseemly."

We inched a little closer to the toll booths.

I said, "Don't you think you were at least half wrong being with that fellow in the rowboat?"

She said, "I do not think there was anything wrong or unseemly or improper for me to be in that rowboat."

We crept closer to the toll booths. I was getting a little hot under the collar. I said, "Do you think you were thirty per cent wrong being in that boat? After all—"

She said, "No. I do not."

She was cool. And I was getting hot under the collar. I was becoming very, very vexed. I said, "Could you have been ten percent wrong being—"

She said, "No."

We were about ten car lengths behind the truck that was paying the toll when I said, "Edy, is it possible that you were at least one percent wrong—?"

She said. "No, Lester. I was not even one tenth of one percent wrong."

By now I was furious. Furious? I was livid.

When we got to about two cars from the toll-taker, I leaned across, opened her door and pushed her out. I locked the door behind her.

She stood there open-mouthed. I eased past her and she caught up, trotting alongside the car and yanking on the door handle.

And I shouted to her, "In your wildest imagination, were you one millionth of a trillionth per cent wrong?"

"Absolutely not," was the response.

Incensed, enraged, exasperated and fuming, I paid the toll and left her on the Jersey side of the tunnel.

By the time I got to our apartment, I was so livid that I threw my things into a suitcase and left. This was it. How could a person be so goddammed stubborn?

As I stepped out of the elevator, there she was, paying off a taxi driver and walking into the lobby of the apartment house.

I decided to give her one more chance. Why, I don't know.

I said, "Edy, this is the last time I'm going to ask you. Were you—?"

"No, no, no, no, no," she said adamantly.

I left the building in a fury.

Three weeks later, she went to Tijuana, Mexico and got a divorce.

I didn't contest anything. It was final. I gave her everything. The bankbook, the furniture, my favorite easy chair, everything. Just to be rid of her.

The next day—the very next day—Edy married the fellow in the rowboat.

I always knew why the lady of justice is blindfolded.

But blind?

Mel Brooks, Gofer - 1953

But I'm getting ahead of myself. Let me tell you how I ended up on *The Today Show*. It's years earlier, 1953 to be precise, and I'm on my knees, begging for my old job back with the best known talent agency in the world, the William Morris Agency. They said okay.

One of our clients was Mel Brooks. Yes, that Mel Brooks. Except when I first met him years earlier he was working for a Borscht Belt comic and sax player called Sid Caesar.

Mel's job description was "Gofer."

"Hey, Mel! Gofer coffee."

"Gofer tuna sandwiches, one with mayonnaise, one without."

"Gofer Sid's suits at the cleaners."

"Gofer more coffee, two with milk, one with sugar."

Mel was the star gofer.

Here I am, eight years later, thinking I'm a big shot because the second time around I have a secretary who could be my very own gofer.

Mel and I just stood there looking at one another. Neither one of us knew what to do. I broke the ice. "How long have you been in show business?" I asked.

"About three months," was the answer.

"What have you been doing for three months?"

"Sorting mail in the mailroom."

"Can you take dictation?"

"I can write fast."

"How about typing?"

"I'm learning it now."

"Do you know where to get coffee?"

"I think so."

My secretary, Bernie Weintraub, had not yet achieved Mel's level of natural ability.

I pulled out a dollar. "Go get us two cups," I said.

Mel had refined his gofer skills in the Catskills. He'd been a "tummeler." Ever heard the word? Well, the Encarta® *World English Dictionary, North American Edition* says it's a noun. That much you probably figured out already. Then it says the definition is "man entertainer; a man employed as a comedian and host to encourage audience participation, especially one hired to amuse guests at resorts in the Catskill Mountains, north of New York City."

Can you think of a better training ground for working with a bunch of crazy comedians? Mel did whatever it took to make those vacationing families laugh. He jumped in the pool with his clothes on. He acted out idiot parts in the sketches. He set up chairs in the casino. And he met Sid Caesar, who was the band leader, sax player, and emcee at a "cook-for-thyself" party in South Fallsburg, New York.

It was love at first skit.

Mel followed Sid around, running errands and howling at his jokes and antics. He always egged Sid on and Mel's genuine glee cued the audience as to what was going to happen, ratcheting up the hilarity factor.

Lots of hilarity translated to lots of attention. Out of nowhere, Max Leibman, a world class producer (with the world's worst hairpiece), asked Sid to star in an hour and a half TV program with Imogene Coca, Carl Reiner, and Howie Morris. Mel knew a good thing when he saw it, so he trailed along, hoping that the superstar producer would eventually recognize his talent and possibly allow him, Mel Brooks, to become a writer for the new show.

What does all this have to do with me? Well, somebody, somehow, had signed Mel as a client of the Morris office. It must have been as a favor to Sid because, I mean, what does an agent do for a gofer? Even though they made big salaries, writers and directors for television (who represented all of my clients) were at the bottom of the status totem pole. Where exactly did that put an ex-tummeler?

Bernie and I knew about Mel's burning desire to be a writer. So we treated him as we would any of the writers, with the same level of deference and courtesy the rest of the industry accorded the profession. Which is to say, not so much.

But word started to get around. Mel's antics were attracting attention. The guy was funny and Carl Reiner and the writers recognized it.

It takes a bunch to know one, so Larry Gelbart (who would go on to write *M.A.S.H.* and several motion pictures as well as Broadway shows), and another comic writing genius, Neil Simon, who would one day become America's most prolific and successful playwright, thought he was mad as a hatter. Just like them. Carl Reiner, the comic who developed into a great actor and director and who one day would join

Mel in a series of side-splitting albums, including *The Thousand Year Old Man* also realized Mel was the real deal along with Mel Tolkin the head writer, Shelly Keller and the others. Then Woody Allen, whose short stories, plays and movies would someday make him an American icon and auteur, started to develop a soft spot for the crazy guy who would stop at nothing to make him laugh.

And then one day, it happened. Just like that. From fetching coffee and cream soda to full-fledged, ingenious creator of masterful monologues and sketches. Mel was a writer. But he was still Mel. Eccentric, and I'm guessing, ADD to the *n*th degree in a world that didn't even know what Attention Deficit Disorder meant.

Somewhere in Mel's brain, becoming a writer and being late for work correlated as appropriate behavior.

So he did.

Come in late.

All the time.

Carl and the writers were livid.

Mel would offer creative alibis and if they didn't work, he'd outright lie.

One day Mel was two hours late. Carl was by now peeved. The writers were furious.

In addition to the fact that Sid no longer had a gofer, the eccentric and inexplicable behavior of a guy who had only been a writer for six months was insulting.

Let's face it, Mel had become a giant pain in the ass.

A room full of grumbling writers and performers jumped three feet when the office door banged open. Racing in at breakneck speed, was a breathless Mel Brooks sporting a straw hat. Everyone turned to holler at him. They were mad as hell.

But Mel went into comic overdrive. Flinging his straw hat across the room, he screamed, "Lindy made it!" The self-reference was hysterical. Everybody cracked up. Something shifted and from then on Mel Brooks became an indispensable originator of incredible wit, timing and fun.

If I had a time machine, I'd take you back with me to those Monday morning writer's meetings. You would die laughing. The man just had a comic aura; before he even started, people were smiling in anticipation. It was one of those you-had-to-be-there things, but if you've seen *The Producers* on Broadway, *Blazing Saddles*, *Space Balls*, *The History of the World, Part I*, *High Anxiety*, *Young Frankenstein*, or any of his other brilliant work, I bet you can imagine it. The incredible mind and mouth of the guy created magic and everyone, Carl included, was helpless in his presence.

Sid Caeser was working on a monologue about a fly. He had barely mentioned the word "fly" before Mel jumped on to the middle of the conference table.

Suddenly he was the leader of a squadron of houseflies descending on a juicy piece of bread and jam. Arms out, buzzing loudly, broken field running around the coffee cups, he yelled, "Chickie, everybody, someone's coming. Quick, make like you're a raisin!" And he abruptly dropped on the table in a fetal position.

Mel made my days as an agent, and the nights of Carl Reiner and the cast, brighter. I take that back. Not brighter - hilariously joyful.

I can recall that night of nights, when I was at a retirement party for the aforementioned Harry Kalcheim, an agent extra-ordinaire. The master of ceremonies, Carl Reiner, one of the captains of comic hilarity, turned to me on the dais, the last one among the many luminaries, and called me to the microphone.

How could I forget?

He said the words, "I would now like you to meet one of the funniest men in show business, Lester Colodny."

That was the way he introduced me.

Carl Reiner. The man who performed beside the great Sid Caeser, in side-splitting sketches and interviews and who made the world laugh till their sides hurt.

Carl Reiner.

Himself.

I sat there, open-mouthed, stunned, and as the applause ebbed, I stood up, tottered to the microphone, bowed to Mr. Reiner, and in absolute happiness and sheer exultation, ad-libbed a speech that made his words ring true.

Oh Carl, that you should have touched me twice so that my life would have changed. For the better? I know not.

After a sensational run on *Your Show of Shows*, one of the biggest television shows of its day, Mel was flying high. He was a wanted commodity. He had transformed from gofer to writer and director nonpareil.

The Polly Bergen Show was a summer replacement show. Polly was a well-known star, so the project had real possibilities. I sold Polly and her manager on the idea of Mel as producer, director and writer.

Mel had Polly's number in a heartbeat. He thought in her "voice," which is what incredibly gifted professionals do. Just about everything that Polly said on air came out of Mel's typewriter.

After four weeks, the sponsors picked up the option on the show for nine additional shows and Polly's manager, Freddie Fields (later her husband) called to make me an offer of five thousand dollars a week for Mel for the rest of the summer.

Five thousand dollars a week! For someone who had been a gofer making fifty bucks just a few years ago?

"Call Mel," I said to my secretary. Bernie dialed.

I picked up the phone and told Mel about Freddie's offer.

"What do you think?" I asked him.

"What do I think, Lester? What do you think? You're the agent," Mel said.

"Not nearly enough," I said.

"Five thousand a show? That's forty-five thousand bucks!"

I said, "Well, I think I can get you more."

"Okay," Mel said. "I leave it to you. But please, don't blow it."

"Get me Freddie," I said to Bernie.

Bernie dialed.

I picked up the phone and said, "Not enough money, Freddie."

"Five thousand a show isn't enough?" Freddie said sarcastically. "How about seven-five?"

"I'll have to get back to you."

I looked around for Bernie.

There was a note on my desk: "Had to go to the bathroom." So I called Mel myself.

"Mel? I told you. They offered seven thousand five hundred."

"Lester, take it. Take it."

"I can get you more."

"But Lester, seven-five?"

"I think I've got him on the hook," I said. "I'll call you back."

"All right, but please, don't louse this up," Mel begged.

I hung up and called Freddie Fields. "Still not enough, Freddie," I said. "He's hot. Mel is real hot. There are three shows panting for him as we speak."

"Then how much do you want?" Freddie asked.

I took a deep breath and said, "He gets ten thousand or he walks."

I had the balls of an elephant.

"Ten thousand?" Freddie gasped. "That's a lot of dough for a summer show."

"That's a lot of talent," I said shot back. Freddie Fields was dumbfounded by the number. I could tell. Ten thousand dollars, even to produce, direct and write, was unprecedented for a summer replacement program.

Unprecedented? It was astronomical.

"I'll have to have a talk with Polly," Freddie said.

But I happened to know that Freddie knew that Polly couldn't say "'boo'" without Mel writing and directing it.

I was so full of myself I could feel my head swelling. I called Mel.

"Mel," I said, "I just spoke to Freddie Fields. And I stuck it up his behind. I stuck an umbrella in his ass and opened it. I stuck it up so far that—"

A voice said, "Who is this?"

"Mel?" I whispered.

"No. It's Freddie Fields."

My head exploded.

"And Mr. Colodny," Fields continued, "you might be a great agent someday, if you ever learn to dial a phone."

When my secretary got back from the men's room I yelled, "Where the bloody hell were you?"

"They ran out of toilet paper," he said.

But we got the ten thousand. For nine shows. I was mortified about what had happened, but the show was a smash. The story went around the New York television establishment like wildfire. But instead of being crucified, I was deified. Before I knew it, I became The Agent. I was made.

"Did you hear about Mel Brooks?"

"What happened?"

"Colodny of the Morris office got him ten thou a show for the *Polly Bergen Show*."

Not a whisper of the imbecilic phone call. All anybody cared about was how much money had changed hands. From then on, everyone who produced a television comedy show took my calls.

I sold six writers to the Red Buttons Show; Marvin Marx and Walter Stone to The Jackie Gleason Show; and I put together an entirely new writing staff for The Milton Berle Show. There was no stopping me.

This agent stuff with William Morris was seriously fun. As soon as I signed a writer, I sold him to someone. Or some show. Or some project. It was exhilarating.

For a while, that is. Because the truth is, I was a wannabe. I wanted to be where my writers were. I wanted to be a comedy writer who got screams from the audiences.

At night I worked on scripts. For shows. For series. For Broadway. Even for. . .deep breath. . .Hollywood.

A Really Big Shoo

I was determined to become a professional writer. One who was paid for writing, not dialing the phone.

In the meantime, I learned an important secret: television comedians had little patience with comedy writers. They were always firing old ones and hiring new ones. As soon as a writer, or a whole team of writers, was let go, I immediately started hunting down new jobs for them as well as new writers to fill their old jobs.

The same thing held true for comedy directors. Television comedians were a persnickety bunch. Lots of attitude, lots of arrogance. If a line or a sketch didn't get a laugh, it certainly wasn't their fault. "Off with their heads!" was the rallying cry from the top stars of the day. Business was booming.

One day Larry Aurback, a fellow agent, was vacationing in Canada and saw the work of a brilliant young director, Norman Jewison. He brought him in and I got him a staff job at CBS. Then I spotted Paul Mazurski who was doing great work off Broadway, and got him into directing television. Herb Ross, director for Barbara Streisand's *Funny Lady*, struck me as someone who would be a first rate director for TV (and later film). I made it so.

I was, in spite of myself, becoming a first rate agent and my ego was expanding accordingly.

One day, I got an order for a Hollywood director. It was from Marlo Lewis, the executive producer of *The Ed Sullivan Show*, which was the number one show at CBS.

I had been after Marlo for months, trying my damnedest to sell him something, anything. One morning, after I'd been following him around like a puppy, Marlo turned to me and said, "Alright, Colodny. Get me a Hollywood director for the Ed Sullivan summer replacement show."

He and Ed Sullivan were represented by one of the biggest agencies in the business, MCA, Music Corporation of America. The agency represented all kinds of directors—especially Hollywood directors! And here he was asking me to get him a Hollywood director.

I couldn't believe my ears. He wanted the William Morris office to get him a director? It was unheard of.

Marlo said, "I want a first rate director, with film experience. I'll pay ten thousand a week, for thirteen weeks, two weeks of prep at full pay. That's fifteen weeks, and we'll put him up at the Plaza Hotel, all expenses paid plus air fare. But he's got to be real good. Really, really, good."

I was elated.

Elated? I was inflated. I had cracked CBS big time. And what a deal. A hundred fifty thousand! For the summer, yet. Plus all expenses paid. I had my secretary, Bernie Weintraub, rush a teletype (grandfather to the fax machine) to our West Coast office, requesting the bios of all of the top Hollywood directors. We gave them the parameters in no uncertain terms.

At the end of the teletype message I said, "First rate, he's gotta be first rate. With lots of screen credits. No prima donnas. Good guy, easy going is important. But he has to be tops."

Ten minutes later, I received a message back. "Have the perfect director for Sullivan replacement show: Lem Ayers available. He is absolutely tops. See book for bio."

Bernie and I looked up Lem Ayers in the office book. He had scads of credits—*Ziegfeld Follies*, *Kiss Me Kate* and much more.

I called Marlo at the *Sullivan Show* and told him I could deliver Lem Ayers.

"Lem Ayers, Lem Ayers, ringing a bell. Remind me. What has he done?" Marlo asked.

I read off his credits.

"Ohhhh! That Lem Ayers. Good job, you've got a deal. Have him report here, to me, at CBS in three weeks. I'll have my secretary book his hotel reservations."

Incredible. Just like that. Sold.

Fantastic. Sensational.

Weintraub and I hugged one another and jumped up and down. We had sold a director to an MCA show. It was the coup of coups.

I had Bernie send word by teletype that the deal was set. Then we went out and celebrated with a two-martini lunch.

When we got back to the office there was a teletype waiting for us.

"Colodny: Sorry. We made a mistake. Lem Ayers died three months ago."

I had sold CBS, Ed Sullivan and Marlo Lewis a dead director.

I'd said easy-going but even for Hollywood this would have been over the top.

In an unusually high voice I said to Bernie, "You'd better get me Marlo Lewis."

Bernie could get no further than Marlo's secretary.

"Lester has got to talk with Mr. Lewis right away. It's imperative," he said.

I could feel the blood draining out of my head and my chest, pooling at my feet. "It's just the martinis," I told myself. "You can handle this."

Marlo's secretary said, "He told me that he was not to be disturbed. Sorry."

"You don't understand—" Bernie said.

"Sorry." Click.

Bernie gave me a look. "I think you better get over there and track him down. Personally."

"I think you're right," I responded and took off running.

I probably looked like a semaphore on steroids as I waved frantically to hail a cab. Finally, one of them took pity on me and off we went to CBS.

Marlo was producing the last *Ed Sullivan Show* of the season. When he took a break, I whispered, "Marlo, I have to talk to you."

He said, "We're OK with Lem Ayers, aren't we?"

"That's what I wanted to talk to you about."

At that moment, Ed Sullivan walked by and smiled at both of us.

"Ed is very pleased with Lem Ayers," Marlo said. "Very pleased. Notice how he smiled at you? He never smiles."

"Marlo, I have to talk to you. Now."

"He put it in his column for Monday," Marlo said. "It's syndicated in two hundred papers. By Monday night, the whole world will know that Lem Ayers is directing Ed Sullivan's summer replacement. Congratulations." He clapped me on the back as he turned to walk away.

A lightning bolt. That would work. It would be quick, I wouldn't feel anything. . .please God. . .

"Marlo," I managed to croak.

"What? What is it?" he asked, annoyed that I was still there.

"Marlo. How do I tell you this?"

"Tell me what?"

I whispered to him, "Marlo, Lem Ayers is dead."

"I can't hear you, what?"

I said, as quietly as possible, "Lem Ayers is dead."

Marlo turned to me. "This is your way of telling me that the Morris office doesn't want to sell Mr. Ayers to us, isn't it? You sons of bitches."

"Marlo, Lem Ayers died. Three months ago."

"You want more money, don't you?" Marlo yelled.

"Marlo, will you listen? Lem Ayers is dead. D-e-a-d."

He said, "We have a deal. I don't give a crap if he's dead or alive. Have him here at CBS in three weeks or I'll sue the Morris office for a million dollars."

I rushed back to the office and asked my boss' secretary if she could either get me in to see him or get me a gun to shoot myself with.

She said, somewhat pityingly, "Mr. Kalcheim has a lunch date."

"Believe me, this is important. Very, very important."

"You don't understand, Lester. . ."

"No, you don't understand. Head wounds are messy."

She looked at me reluctantly, then buzzed Kalcheim on the phone. "Les Colodny says he has something very, very important he has to talk to you about right away." She listened a moment, then said to me, "Go on in."

"What's up?" Harry Kalcheim asked.

"Harry, I just sold a director to CBS and—"

"Capital," Harry said. "That's great. Somebody finally broke the damn barrier. MCA's had a monopoly there for years. Who'd you sell the director to?"

"Marlo Lewis."

"Marlo!" Harry said. "The Sullivan show? Wow. Nothing like starting off with a bang."

I winced.

Harry didn't notice. "Congratulations. Who's the director?"

"Lem Ayers."

"Lem Ayers, hmmm. What has he directed?"

I rattled off a list of his credits.

"Oh, you mean Lem Ayers. Swell."

"But there's a problem."

"Problem?"

"Yes. He's dead."

"Dead? I never read that in the trade papers."

I stood my ground. "Nevertheless, he's still dead."

"How do you like that," Harry mused. "Lem Ayers, dead. I'll have to send condolences."

"Harry, I sold him to the Sullivan show. What do I do?"

"What do you mean, 'What do I do?'"

"Harry, he died. He's dead. Buried."

"Buried, not cremated, huh?"

"Harry," I pleaded, "Harry, what do I do with CBS?"

At that moment, Harry's secretary poked her head in the doorway and said, "Your lunch date is here."

"Harry, what do I do?"

Harry said, "You've got a big problem, Lester," and left.

I was shunned. You know, like the Amish do to the damned. It's a punishment reserved for thieves, scoundrels, blackguards and bounders. People don't pretend to ignore you, they literally decide you never existed. They look right through you. They can't hear you.

It's like being in Beetlejuice. You're invisible. Every executive at CBS and everybody at every single one of their affiliates was in on it.

I had my secretary call anybody and everybody I'd ever dealt with to make lunch dates so I could apologize, grovel, do penance. They would show up at the appointed hour with friends and colleagues. They would collectively ignore my pleas for mercy, refuse to acknowledge my very existence, laugh and talk among themselves and then leave. But they let me pay the check.

I took that as a good sign.

The Martian Dialogue

But the pièce de résistance, if one might use that old phrase, the final straw that made me quit the agency, was when the vice president in charge of all programming at NBC, Michael Strasbourg, called me in and said, "Colodny, I'm unhappy with the scripts on *My Favorite Martian*."

The show had been sold and was to go on the next season. The Morris office represented the writer who created the show and had already prepared thirteen scripts.

I said, "What are you unhappy about?"

"I want you to bring in the guys who write this show. I want to talk to them."

"Actually, there are seven writers on the show. Manny is the head writer. You want me to bring in all the writers?"

"All of them," he said.

"Okay. You're the boss."

I went back to the office and had my secretary put in a call to the *My Favorite Martian* office in Beverly Hills. I spoke to Manny Mannheim, the creator of the show and head writer.

"Listen, Manny, the head of programming here in New York is unhappy with the scripts and wants to talk to you guys."

"So let him pick up the phone," he said.

"He wants to talk to each one of you."

"What about?"

"Search me. But come in. What do you have to lose? They'll pay all expenses, you can fly first class, they'll put you up at the Plaza Hotel and you can get to see a few Broadway shows."

"Okay. We'll be in tomorrow."

The next day, I picked up the eight writers at JFK and drove with them to the network. "It's good to see you guys," I said.

"What do you think he's unhappy about?" asked Manny.

"If I knew I'd tell you. Let him tell you himself."

We trooped into the building on Fifty-Second Street and entered the big man's office.

He greeted us and after some small talk, he said, "Look, fellas, I have to tell you, I'm not too happy with the scripts."

"What seems to be the trouble?" asked Manny.

Mr. Strasbourg pointed to a pile of scripts and said, "I have here all the scripts for the first thirteen shows. I'll pick out one. At random."

He poked at the pile and pulled out a script.

"Here," he said, "on page fourteen of this script, number eleven."

He read a line and looked up.

"Now," he said, "a Martian wouldn't say that."

The writers all looked at me and, without a word, left the room.

"Where are they going?" asked the executive.

"Back to California," I said.

Howie's Party - 1952

About this time, I became very friendly with Howard Arnold, a brassiere salesman and a well known man about town. Howie Arnold was God's gift to women. He loved them. And they adored him. There wasn't a model or actress in town that hadn't gone out with Howie. And he had slept with most of them.

So, when he invited me to his birthday party (that he was throwing for himself), I knew that there would be a boat load of gorgeous girls. Maybe I would get lucky.

When I walked in, I gasped. A boat load? It was like a convention of stunning womanhood. The room was filled with fantastic, striking, sensational females.

"Lester," Howie's voice echoed in my ear, "welcome to my party. Have a drink and find yourself a lovely lady."

I walked over to the bartender. "Look, I'm not much of a drinker so make me something light."

"A light what?" he asked.

"A light anything."

As he poured me a drink, I surveyed the room. Never before in my life did I imagine that there were so many beautiful women in New York. Where to start? How to start?

I grabbed the drink and swallowed it in one gulp. And then the room began to swim. "What did you put in that drink?" I demanded of the bartender.

"I thought you were kidding, sir. That was a triple bourbon and soda."

I made my way to a couch and sat down between two outstanding women. They were amazingly gorgeous. They were discussing something but who cared. I just sat there and stared. I was half drunk but I was in pig heaven.

When a waiter came by, I ordered another triple bourbon. What the hell? And I started to get into the discussion. Three drinks later, I was reeling but having a great time.

Howie came over and asked, "How're you doing?"

I mumbled something about never wanting to go home and coming to live with him. He smiled and moved on to another group.

It was at that moment that I spilled my drink on the redhead next to me. All over her dress. She jumped to her feet.

I looked up at her slightly cross-eyed and said abjectly, "I beg your pardon, Miss O'Hara."

She was soaking wet. "Who?"

I said, "I'm sorry, I could have sworn you were Maureen O'Hara," as I clumsily dabbed at her with my handkerchief. That was the last thing I remember.

I awoke with a tremendous hangover. It was like a black cloud that enveloped my entire body. I raised my head and looked around. It was then that I saw, through what looked like a cloud of smoke that seemed to envelop me, the redhead coming toward me with a cup of something.

"Here, drink this," she said.

As I drank the dreadful concoction, I said, "What happened last night?"

She said, "The doorman and the cab driver had to drag you up three flights of stairs. Now I have to go home."

"Oh my God," I said remembering to shake my pounding head very slowly. "Did I say anything, do anything, you know, to embarrass you?"

"No. In fact, I liked being thought of as Maureen O'Hara."

"Maureen O'Hara?" I said.

"That's what you called me. You said, 'Excuse me, Miss O'Hara.'"

"I didn't," I said, holding my throbbing head in my hands.

"Then you proposed," she said.

"Was it something indecent?" I asked sheepishly.

"You asked me to marry you."

"Oh no," I said. "I am so sorry. Look, I'm not used to drinking. In fact, I never drink. I don't know what came over me. Please forgive me."

"What for?" She smiled. It was the sweetest smile. "Oh," she said as she paused in the doorway, "I might just take you up on that proposal." She reached for the handle to close the door behind her. "By the way. My name is Dee. Dee Masterson."

The door closed, very quietly.

Three months later, we were married at the church on Fifth Avenue and Fifty-Fifth Street. It was Episcopalian, which we figured was sort of half way between Jewish and Catholic. We planned a small wedding with twenty or so friends and family. It was going to be in a small side alcove and we were going out to lunch afterwards.

Somebody came and whispered something to the minister, who looked at us and crooked his finger. Mystified, we followed him.

There in the main vestibule of the church were hundreds, I'm telling you hundreds of people. Everybody I knew, and a bunch I didn't, had crashed the wedding. Somehow word went around, "Hey, did you hear? Colodny is getting married. Let's go."

It was unbelievable. It was as if anybody in town even remotely connected with show business had come to the ceremony. Everybody from William Morris, along with their wives and secretaries, writers, directors, friends, and neighbors, were there. Every client I represented was sitting there cheering. You wouldn't believe the cast of characters, from stars to office boys.

You should have seen the look on Dee's face. Can you imagine? It was indescribable. I was so thrilled, so flattered I thought I was going to expire from happiness. So after the ceremony (which was punctuated with one-liners from the spontaneous peanut gallery that had assembled), I wondered, now what?

We had lunch planned for twenty. What were we going to do with this crowd?

But these were show folk, and they always rise to the occasion. Milton Berle raced to the Stage delicatessen and bought just about every morsel of food in the place. Four or five others did the same with their favorite lunch spots and we took over a huge suite at the old Knickerbocker hotel. What a raucous, rowdy, hysterical celebration it was.

How do you top that?

Howie found a way. While the festivities were still going on, he handed me two first class tickets to Las Vegas. Dee and I flew off to Nevada for our honeymoon and were toasted all the way to the airport in the longest limousine available.

That night, in Milton Berle's private cabana at the El Rancho Vegas, in Nevada, Kim Elizabeth Colodny was conceived.

Living with the Stars

The Colodnys were living the good life. I had some money in the bank. We bought a big old house near the Triborough Bridge in Whitestone, with sixteen rooms. We had a live in maid and a nanny for Kim. And soon, Kathleen Jill Colodny came along.

I was riding high, and our home became a haven for every kind of show business talent there was. Every weekend there was a luncheon, a dinner or a party at our house.

The guest list looked like a who's who in the entertainment world. From Dick Cavett to Ella Fitzgerald, Julius La Rosa to Sara Vaughn, Neil Simon, Larry Gelbart, Mel Brooks, Milton Berle, Red Buttons, Sid Caesar, Imogene Coca, actors, musicians, designers, lighting and sound people, network executives; you name them, they were all there.

Drinking, eating, exchanging lies and gossip, singing, telling jokes. It was wonderful.

However, after three and a half years of making obeisance to personalities on the potty and pushing writers and directors for William Morris, I was getting tired of selling everybody except Lester Colodny.

One day I heard about a job opening at NBC. It was for the manager of new comedy writer development, a brand new idea for the network to come up with fresh young talent. I applied for the job.

I'll never forget the interview. It was with Richard A.R. Pinkham, a man who went on to become one of the prime movers and shakers in the advertising business.

I sat across from him in a huge NBC office and he said to me,

"Well, young man, what do you want to be when you grow up?"

Just like that.

I responded with the first thing that came to my mind. I said, "I'd like your job."

The next thing I knew, I had quit William Morris and I had become the manager of New Comedy Writer Development at NBC, in an office the size of my closet, filled with scripts from would-be comedy writers.

After reading hundreds of scripts I hired, among others, Shelly Berman (who went on to become a famous stand up comic); Paul Keyes (who became the head writer and producer of *The Jack Paar Show*), Herb Hartig (who became Sid Caesar's stand-in on *Your Show Of Shows* and one of the two comics in a team of "Igor and I" with Paul Mazursky, the film director); Bruce Howard (who became one of the key writers of the TV series *The Dukes Of Hazzard*); Herb Reich (my former partner); Lois Korey (who became one of the most famous writers of commercials and ads and my life-long friend); and a young wisp of a joke writer named Alan Koenigsberg (who developed into one of the great writers and directors of the twentieth and twenty-first centuries, Mr. Woody Allen).

I also had the opportunity to hire experienced writers to work with the young hopefuls. It was a grand and glorious time.

Then things in New York began to dry up. I don't know why but all the work seemed to be in California. I talked NBC into trying an experiment. I took all of our writers, the old and the new, and my wife Dee who was now very pregnant with number three, and we embarked for Hollywood and Colodny's Brilliant Enterprise.

In California, ensconced at the Hollywood Hawaiian Motel, I made the rounds of all the comedy and variety shows, using the art of persuasion that I had learned at the William Morris Agency, and one by one, placed every one of my writers. It was a huge success. They acquitted themselves with glory.

But there was one thing I hadn't considered. Every one of my writers was put on a major show. And that left me without a job. I returned to New York and begged my way back into the good graces of Harry Kalcheim, my boss, and the William Morris Agency for another three long years.

That was my first big mistake.

But there was good news too. Because tiny Mace Matthew Colodny showed up, squawking and gurgling and we were five. It was all wonderful.

And then Dee began to pout. "What's the matter?" I asked her.

"Nothing."

The next day it was the same thing. "Come on, tell me. Something's eating at you."

"There's nothing eating at me."

"Then why have you been so. . .so. . .so morose lately. Where's that Dee that I used to love so much?"

"Yes, where is she?" was the reply.

Uh oh.

It kept getting worse. One day I sat down on the couch and said, "Okay, out with it. You're driving me nuts."

She finally answered, "It's your friends."

"My friends?"

"All those people who congregate here every week."

"You're talking about all the show business people?" I asked her.

"Yes. They're all. . ."

"All what?"

"They're all phonies."

I was aghast. "Phonies? Who's a phony? Neil Simon is a phony? Mel Brooks is a phony? Milton Berle is a phony?"

"All they do is show off," she said.

"They are not showing off," I answered. "They're being themselves among themselves."

"All they do is top one another. One tells a joke and the next one tells another joke and—"

"Dee, that's the way people in the business ease off. That's relaxation for them. When Ella gets up to sing for everyone, it's not for anyone except herself. She's letting it all hang out."

"Well, I don't like them. I'm sick and tired of them. To be perfectly honest, they bore me to tears."

I was stunned. "What are you talking about?" I said. "We're the toast of New York!"

"All they want is work from you. We're just toast," she said.

I stared at her in disbelief.

"Lester, grow up. These people don't give a damn who or what you are. They just found a convenient place to hang out."

I loved every moment of it. The kids loved it. I reveled in it and my wife reviled it.

The Anti-Gravity Machine - 1960

So what was life like on *The Today Show*? Is it really a crazy business?

I was in the office of a friend, Shad Northshield, the executive producer of *The Today Show*. He had heavy dark bags under his eyes.

"What's the matter, Shad?" I asked him.

"Dave Garroway. He's at it again."

"What is it this time?"

"He wants to open the show tomorrow with another nut case. You won't believe this—he has a guy who's invented an anti-gravity machine."

"A what?"

"That's what I said. It's another of Dave's crackpot inventor buddies. Dave wants to open the show and tell the audience about this guy and his crazy machine. Dave will weigh himself. Then he'll put on this gizmo and get on the scale again and we'll see that he weighs thirty pounds less."

"You've got to be kidding me."

"That's what he tells me."

"Maybe it'll work."

"Maybe? We interview statesmen, politicians, movie stars, important people on this show. We can't have lunatics with whacky ideas on the show, just because they're friends of our nut-bar star."

At the time, I was an agent for the William Morris Agency. I sold writers to televisions programs. I realized this was probably not the most propitious moment to bring the subject up but I decided to go for it anyway. "Shad," I said, "I have a writer for you."

"I don't need a writer. I need a keeper for Dave."

"This guy is terrific."

"Lester, I don't need a writer."

"This writer is not only fast, he's concise and was the champion précis writer in his class."

"Précis champion? That's what we can use around here. A person who can write précis of the news. How did you know?"

"I watch the show every morning, that's how. And I listen to Dave always cutting into those long newscasts."

"Who is this writer?"

"Me."

"You? You're selling me you? What happened at the agency?"

"I quit."

"Tell me," he said with a smile.

I shrugged and looked at Shad, hoping he would understand. "First Freddie Fields and Mel Brooks. Then the dead director. But a vice president who knew what Martians would say? It was too much. Besides, I never wanted to be an agent. So there it is. What about that job as précis writer?"

Shad looked at me and smiled.

He said, "When do you want to start?"

So, that's how I got started and fired at *The Today Show*. As I am sure you will agree, the maniacal monkeys weren't my fault. It was just one of those things.

Later, Dave Garroway suffered a personal tragedy and lost interest in the show. The network replaced everybody on the show. At this point, Madam Fate stepped in again, this time to prove that Dee was right.

It was the end of my show business career in New York.

I went around to Berle and to Buttons and to the writers and musicians and people I had met on *The Today Show*, looking for work. Anything, associate producer, writer, assistant, but it was as if I had never existed.

What happened to me?

From being a co-producer of a two-hour, daytime television show, on speaking terms with stars, statesmen, politicians, authors, and public figures from every walk of life, suddenly I was out of a job. I was through. Washed up. Finished.

I didn't even cast a shadow any longer.

I had been a good producer. A hell of a producer. I did a great job on the show.

So why wasn't anyone taking my calls anymore?

I had been a respected working member of the New York theatrical community. A wheel. A medium sized wheel, but a wheel nonetheless. I drove the biggest car Chrysler made. I had my own table at Sardi's. I was invited to every opening night and every closing party.

It was "Hi Lester," and "Lester, baby," and Lester, sweetie," and "What can I do for you?" and "What do you need?"

Now, there was just silence.

In the two and a half years that I was producing, had I ever, ever, said "no" to anyone? Had I ever refused a favor to an agent or a manager or a musician or somebody who needed a book plugged or a charity helped or a cause espoused?

"You need something? Call Lester Colodny at NBC. He does the impossible. He's a dreamboat."

I was bereft.

It was no longer, "Lester sweetie, but sorry, Lester."

At least Dee didn't say, "I told you so."

Going to California 1956-57

I was married for the second time. To Dee, with two children—Kim, who was three and Kathy, who was two.

I know. I was one of those people with an urge to be loved. And when I met Dee, at a party thrown by my friend Howard Arnold, I fell instantly, passionately, irreversibly, in lust for her.

Although she wasn't too thrilled by my desire to be in show business, my ardor overcame her protests and I pursued every avenue I could find. But there I was, at the age of thirty-two, with a wife, two children, and one on the way. I'd just been fired from *The Today Show*. I had to do something, anything.

I had an inspiration. (It was really an act of desperation). I called my old friend, Leonard Grainger, who had moved to Los Angeles.

"Leonard," I cried. "Help!"

"What is it?"

"I'm not sure but I think I may have contracted leprosy," I said. "I can't figure this thing out. How can a man with all the friends I had suddenly find himself ostracized?"

"You weren't ostracized, putz, you were fired."

"But how come no one will let me sleep in their doorway?"

"Come out, Lester," he said. "Where the sun shines all day long and you can drink orange juice from the trees."

The rasping voice of the public address system announced the departure of my flight to Los Angeles.

I plodded wearily up to the gate and on to the plane.

I looked around and found that I was seated in the middle of a three-seat section. The seats on either side of mine were unoccupied. That was a break I sorely needed. I pulled the armrests out of their holes and made a narrow bed with two tiny TWA blankets and even tinier TWA pillows. (Who the hell did TWA think flew on their stupid airplanes? Midgets?)

The party was wild. Wall to wall females, as far as the eye could see. I felt like a kid in a candy store who has just been told he can have anything he wants. Free. But there was too much there and I wanted to taste it all

Then I saw her.

Tall and blonde, and stacked up to the ceiling. She had one of those tiny, Irish noses that swept up, and two of the most gorgeous breasts, pointing directly at me. Christ, what legs. They seemed to start from under her armpits. And then she smiled. Right at me.

I looked around to see if perhaps it was someone else she was smiling at. But there was no one behind me. I took one last drag on the cigarette I was smoking, put it out, and finished my drink before looking back at her.

She was still smiling.

I could feel little fingers of excitement running up and down my spine. And then I began to shake and quiver because those long, long, legs were unwinding from around the bar stool and making their way in my direction.

She walked up to me and whispered. . .

"May I have your attention, please."

I jerked awake as though I'd been hit by a cattle prod. It was the captain rudely interrupting my dream (and yes that was the actual dream, no embellishments added).

"We are encountering a slight problem with our landing gear."

I sat bolt upright.

A slight problem with our landing gear? There is no such thing as a slight problem with landing gear. Landing gear either works or it doesn't. The wheels go up and down or they don't go up and down.

You have to be kidding me! I survive the Japanese Air Force, Hitler, the United States Navy, debts, doubts, heartache and broken dreams, and the whole thing is going to be blown on a faulty hydraulic system?

"We're going to circle the airport and they'll tell us whether our landing gear is up or down," said the captain.

We waited, our collective hearts beating so hard I imagined the plane throbbing with fear.

The captain said, "I'm afraid that the landing gear is not down. We may have to make an emergency landing."

An emergency landing. That means with no wheels. (See above.)

So this was it. The sum total of my existence was about to be added up and entered into the big ledger in the sky.

Well, at least I would get to rest. No more scuffling, no more hustling. No necessity of proving to anyone that I was really more than I appeared to be.

I wondered, Tom Sawyer style, if there would be a funeral. A big funeral.

"Did you hear about Lester?"

"Lester who?"

"Colodny. The guy who produced *The Today Show*."

"Colodny? That was the guy killed in the plane crash?"

"Yes."

"No!"

"Now I'll have to cancel that network meeting. Shit. See if you can reschedule it."

"The funeral?"

"No, dummy. The meeting."

I peeked around to make sure the flight attendant was nowhere near and lit a cigarette. I had almost forgotten how delicious a cigarette could taste. Was I ever glad I hadn't quit. Screw the *Reader's Digest* and the American Cancer Society and the Surgeon General. They had never been in a plane about to land without wheels.

A flight attendant appeared at the front of the cabin. She was quite obviously frightened. "Ladies and gentlemen," she said, her voice shaking, "would you please put your heads forward, in your laps."

You've got to be kidding, I thought.

"In the fecal position."

"That's fetal. Fetal," I muttered.

The flight attendant disappeared.

I looked out my window and I could see trucks laying foam along the landing strip and emergency vehicles rushing to the scene. Christ, was I in trouble. We were all in trouble. Behind me somebody had a rosary and was saying her beads. Across the aisle, a man and woman, their eyes closed, were clutching one another.

The plane was getting lower and lower. Now I could see the fire trucks and hoses and dozens of little figures scurrying around. Two of the trucks had a line across a runway. A cable of some sort was attached to the two trucks. Another truck was laying foam on the runway.

Foam.

A woman screamed. Some guy began to sob. The woman behind me fainted dead away. It was like watching a bad B movie. Only I was in it.

It occurred to me that I ought to say a prayer or something. But I couldn't think of one for crash landings. Maybe a hymn might be appropriate. That was it. A hymn. But for the life of me, I couldn't think of one.

Then, all of a sudden, I began to sing:

When the Deep Purple falls,

Over sleepy garden walls,

And the stars begin to flicker in the deep. . .

What a crazy frigging thing to pop into a person's head as he is about to be crushed into a jillion smithereens. Apparently, someone up there must have heard my sixteen bars of "Deep Purple." There was a grinding, wrenching sound from under the fuselage.

"This is your Captain speaking. We have managed to release the landing gear manually and will be landing in Los Angeles shortly. Sorry to have disturbed you."

Sorry to have disturbed me?

I crept back into my tiny TWA pillow and tried to get back to the girl with the legs, but she had already left the party with someone else.

A Funny Thing Happened

Goddamn TWA.

I had left New York and flown to Los Angeles with a heavy heart. No wife, no kids, out here, at least. In California was Leonard Grainger.

Leonard. My savior.

Sure enough, there he was. Steady, reliable, on time. Waiting for me as I came out of the airport. We hugged one another and Leonard held me at arm's length, like a mother seeing her son for the first time after his summer vacation at camp.

"You look like shit," he said.

"Thank you, Leonard."

I'd known Leonard for a decade. And I tried to tell him how much I appreciated his meeting me and taking me in. But Leonard couldn't stand thanks. Or love. Or affection. Thanks and love and affection were only for Leonard to give, as if he had a corner on the market. As if he had been designated as the only dispenser of goodness and truth and sincerity in a bleak, unfeeling world.

Leonard understood human drama. He knew he was looking at a man who had just plummeted from the dizzying heights of success to the bottom of the heap.

"Come," he grinned, "to my palace on the hill. Only one thing, Lester."

"What?"

"Don't get upset. The Grainger Hilton is full up."

That's what his house was called, The Grainger Hilton. Because if you were a friend of Leonard's or even a friend of a friend, there was always a place for you if you were down on your luck. At that moment, there were people sleeping on the couch, on the chairs and even one on the floor of his den.

"Forget it," I said. "I'll stay at a hotel."

Leonard looked at me with a wry smile. "You not only look like shit, you are full of it. You'll stay in my room and I'll sleep on the couch. How is Dee and how are the little ones?"

I started to feel dreadful.

He held up his hand. "Please, you're making me ill. We'll talk about it tonight." Leonard grinned. "I made a great pot roast for dinner."

The trip into Beverly Hills was a blur of sounds and sights. Palm trees and gossip about who was fired and who was working, who was doing whom, and do you remember the night we nearly burned down lower Manhattan, and whatever happened to what's-his-name.

As for the sights, everybody knows the light in California is magical. It made the clean streets sparkle, it danced off the tanned skin of beautiful young girls with long blonde hair, it made the color blue something lovely to look at instead of how I felt.

Finally the drive up the hill, past the Beverly Hills Hotel, where only a few short months ago I had stayed in the biggest suite, all expenses paid by the network, my every need and whim being tended to.

I whimpered internally.

Leonard's house was one of those super-modern A-frames perched precariously over the edge of a magnificent view of the Los Angeles Basin. For years, Leonard claimed he was searching for another place to live because he was certain that one of those flash rainstorms would one night wash him, his pot roasts and his guests down the hill. But for some reason he stayed.

Nobody was as Leonard as Leonard. Administering to the wretched, consoling the forlorn, helping the unemployed, wiping tears, hugging, patting, listening and sometimes hollering. He was incredible. One of the few men I had ever met who really listened. Whether or not he understood was not important. Only the fact that he permitted other people's feelings and thoughts to penetrate through the outer shell of his own ego into his brain.

I don't suppose it really matters what Leonard's reasons were for running this hostel for lost souls. It didn't matter because he did it well. With style and grace and charm and warmth. Without charge or recrimination or question.

His place was crawling with people and when we came in they all stopped what they were doing and stared at me.

"May I have everyone's attention? This is one of my oldest friends, Lester Colodny. From New York."

They all looked up. Then they went back to whatever they were doing. So much for attention.

Suddenly I felt the hairs on my neck prickle and turned around to see a woman approaching us. There was something predatory about her eyes. She looked at me as though she was assessing a cut of meat.

As she spoke, she was eating a sandwich. "Leonard, is this the man you were telling us about?"

"No, Betty, later," he said. "Come, Lester, you'll use my bedroom. Take a shower and shave, you'll feel better."

As we started to walk into Leonard's bedroom, she stopped him. "Is he. . .single?"

"Leave it alone. The man's had a hard week."

"I just asked. He's very attractive."

"Curb your hunger, Betty. Speaking of which, what the hell are you eating?"

"Sardines."

"Oh, blech."

In the bedroom, I sat on the bed. "Was that sardines she was eating?"

"Yes. God, they stink. I hate them."

"Me too. I loathe them."

"A shower and you'll feel good as new," said Leonard, and left.

I sat there, slowly undressing. Then I stepped into the shower and turned the water on. Everything kind of hit me then, the whole unreal, surreal quality of the past months. I zoned out as the needle sharp spray poured down.

"You're using up all the hot water," Leonard bellowed from the other room.

I turned off the shower and stepped out in a cloud of steam. Groping, I found the towel and started to wipe.

"Oh, Lester, you are so gorgeous."

I stopped dead in my tracks with water running down my body. I smelled her before I saw her.

Betty. Still chomping on that sardine sandwich.

She was coming toward me, unbuttoning her blouse with one hand and eating the last of the sandwich with the other.

I backed away. I didn't want her to touch me with those stinking fingers.

"Leonard," I shouted. Where the hell was Leonard?

She had her blouse off now and was unzipping her skirt with a weird, lusting look in her eyes. My back was against the drapes and I realized that I was on the verge of being groped by a complete stranger. A crazy lady who reeked of sardines.

Groped? She was almost stark naked now, coming closer and closer.

She was intent on fucking me.

I looked wildly around for an exit. Any exit. But she had me cornered between the commode and the sink. In a flash, I ducked under her breasts, wrenched the sliding door open and leaped out onto the small balcony.

A cold rain had replaced the California sunshine. I was naked and wet but I slammed the slider shut behind me.

The door to the bedroom burst open and Leonard entered. Taking in the entire scene in a single glance, he screamed, "You stupid idiotic bitch. All you can think of is screwing. No wonder your husband threw you out on your ass."

Then he saw me standing naked on the tiny patio. "Oh, Lester," he mouthed, "I am so sorry."

He ran to the door and tried to open it but I had slammed it so hard that the lock had broken off. The door was stuck.

"Help, Leonard," I wailed. "I'm freezing to death."

"Try climbing over the far side of the patio and reach for the next door. It isn't far. I'll go get a ladder."

I looked down. The house was built over a steep hill. If I slipped, I was done for.

Leonard came out onto the patio. He had a ladder and when he finally found a piece of dry ground, he propped it up and called to me. Slowly I climbed up on the ledge and edged myself forward, inch by inch. I felt like one of those characters in all the smarmy stories I had ever read as I reached for the ladder.

By now, the rain had turned to icy pellets. As I began my descent to the bottom of the ladder the hail was hitting my bare backside with all the force of an angry farmer's shotgun.

And just as I was about to reach the bottom, the ground gave way and the ladder slid sideways.

I went tumbling down the hill, in the mud and the water, ass over tea kettle, down and down and down, trying to grab onto little tufts of undergrowth that gave way, until I came to rest, stunned and naked, in the back yard of a cottage at the bottom of the hill.

There I lay, semi-conscious, trying to catch my breath, when the back door of the cottage opened and two very pretty blond young men stepped out to survey what all the ruckus was about and what, in addition to the hail, had fallen out of the sky onto their peony bushes.

They took one look at me splayed out in my muddy birthday suit, and then at one another.

"Well," said one of them, "we can wash him up and have him for dinner."

"Who says there's no God," the other one giggled.

Leonard, who had watched in horror as the ladder collapsed, knew he couldn't stop my tumble. He'd grabbed a sheet and come sliding down the mountainside to save me.

Wrapping me in it he wiggled his hips and prissily staked his claim.

"Sorry, boys," he said, "This one is mine."

After Dinner Mintz

A few days later, Leonard and I were sitting over coffee. He was reading the trades and I was looking out the window disconsolately.

"What am I going to do about employment, Leonard? I have to find a job. I've tried just about every place in town. Every film studio, every TV outlet. You told me there were jobs. There are no jobs. What will I tell Dee?"

Leonard put down his paper. "That is pure crap. You're just running into bad luck. Who have you tried?"

"I used your little black book. I called everyone in there."

"Wait a second. I have a name that isn't in that book. Try Morty Mintz at Paramount."

"Morty Mintz?"

"Some people say he's a degenerate. He crash-diets, does drugs, drinks to excess. But he knows everybody on the Paramount lot. And he owes me a favor. I'll call him. Who knows? Maybe he'll know of something. Go. Take my car."

"You think there's a chance?"

"Who knows?"

"Leonard, how do I thank you? You've put up with so much from me."

"Lester, please. You're making me nauseous."

"I'm here to see Morty Mintz. Name is Colodny," I said into the intercom at the producer's home.

One day, I vowed to myself, I'll have a place like this.

I rang the bell and waited. No one answered. I was about to leave when a pretty girl came to the door, adjusting her blouse and skirt.

"Can I help you?" she asked.

Oh for God's sake, I thought. "I'm here to see Mr. Mintz," I said She leaned down and pressed an intercom. "Morty, there's a. . ." she looked up at me questioningly.

"Colodny. Leonard Grainger referred me."

"Leonard?" Into the phone she said, "Sweetheart, Leonard sent him." To me she said, "Go right through the first door on your left, honey." She winked.

When I walked in Morty Mintz was stuffing his shirt into his trousers. Oh for God's sake.

"Sit down, I just had to go to the can," said Mr. Mintz.

Such idiocy.

"What can I do for you?" asked the ostensibly just relieved producer.

"I'm looking for a job. . .any kind of job. Anything."

"Anything?"

"Yes."

"You write, don't you?"

"That's what I do best."

"Fast?"

"Uh-huh."

"How fast?"

"I'm fast. Real fast."

"How about a screenplay? By Monday at nine."

"A whole screenplay by Monday? Today is Friday."

"I got a problem. I got Jack Lemmon on the hook until Monday at nine. I got a screenplay that's dreck. You know what dreck is?"

"I know what dreck is."

"Only this is worse."

"It's garbage?"

"Even worse."

"And you want me to rewrite it. How do you know I can do it?"

"I don't. But Leonard said you're the fastest writer in the world."

"Leonard exaggerates a little."

"You wanna try? I'll pay you five thousand bucks if you finish it by Monday at nine and ten thousand more if Lemmon says it's a go."

Five thousand bucks. Five thousand! But to write an entire screenplay by Monday? It was impossible.

"I don't know," I said.

"Well? Make up your mind. I have to find a writer. Yes or no?"

I thought I might as well take a shot at it. I had nothing to do between now and Monday morning. "I'll do it," I said.

Mintz handed me a script.

"What happens if I don't make it by nine?" I asked.

He shrugged.

As I left the house, I saw his secretary walking back into his office. She was removing her skirt. Oh for God's sake.

I shook my head. That's Hollywood.

"By Monday?" Leonard squeaked.

"I have to deliver it by nine a.m."

"Well, there's only one thing to do."

"What's that?"

"Start writing. Real fast."

About midnight, I stopped to take a breather. There were pages everywhere. Pages on the floor. On the desk.

Leonard was plying me with Benzedrine and coffee.

"It's impossible," I moaned.

"Why?"

"Because this script is unworkable. It doesn't make any sense."

"Then why don't you substitute one of your scripts for this one. Just change the names of the characters and change the venues," Leonard suggested.

"Not enough."

"Then make whatever changes in your script that will fit the bill."

I said to him, "You know, you really are a saint."

"Yeah, yeah, Saint Leonard. The patron saint of job seekers. Just type."

"Yes, sir," I said.

Leonard was dozing in the living room at eight next morning when I walked in with a sheaf of papers in my hand.

"It's done. Finished," I yelled.

Leonard grabbed his keys and we flew out to his car.

"Don't you want to know if it's any good?" I asked.

"Who cares? We have exactly fifty-five minutes. Let's go."

We drove down the freeway, passing cars like we were on the Indianapolis Speedway.

"Leonard, if the cops stop us you'll do five to ten."

"Fuck them," he shouted over the roar of the motor. "We're going to sell this fucking script."

He drove up to the house in Bel Air and yelled into the speaker on the gate, "Open, we got four minutes!"

A voice said, "To see who?"

"Donald Duck. Open. Immediately."

The gate opened and we drove in at sixty miles an hour. I leaped out of the car.

"Good luck and break a leg," Leonard shouted as I rushed up the front stairs and pressed the bell.

I waited. Five minutes. Ten minutes.

What the hell was going on?

I looked at my watch. One minute to nine. To hell with protocol. I burst through the front door and ran into Mintz's office.

Morty Mintz was sitting behind his desk.

"It's one minute to nine. I made it," I said.

I threw the script on his desk and sat down in the chair opposite him. I was out of breath but I was excited as can be. I had finished the script and gotten it to the producer in time to get it to Jack Lemmon and I couldn't wait for him to tell me what a crackerjack job I had done. My first screenplay assignment and I had made it. I was exultant.

But Morty Mintz didn't move.

"Aren't you going to call Lemmon?" I said.

He still didn't move.

Then, from under his desk, the secretary appeared. She had a napkin in her hand.

Without a word she reached for the phone and dialed.

"Is this the Bel Air Police? I think you'd better send an ambulance to Morty Mintz's home. I think he may be dead."

"You think he's dead?" I screeched. "You think he's dead?"

"Yes, I think so," she said.

She reached down with one hand to feel his pulse and with the other pulled up the zipper on his pants.

(I know this sounds callous and unfeeling but Jesus Christ! You can't make this stuff up.)

I said, "You mean to tell me that I stayed up for an entire weekend, and he dies getting his—"

"Please," she said. "Have a little respect."

I picked up my script and headed blindly for the door. No producer. No star. No picture. Nothing.

I was back to where I started. With a script that no one would understand and an unconscious producer who was probably dead.

I couldn't believe what had just happened to me.

In the car, I told Leonard what happened with Morty Mintz.

"Poor guy," he said, "a slave to his hormones."

"What about me?" I complained. "I'm delirious from no sleep and I'm stuck with a mish-mosh of a script and no job. What do I do?"

"You're alive, Lester."

"Yeah, sure."

Finally, I said, "I wonder if they allow oral sex in hell?"

Leonard said, "I think they do at the Writers' Guild."

A Sellers Market

I finished the rewrite of the rewrite of the rewritten version of the script, the one that I had written for Morty Mintz, after rewriting my own. And Leonard was reading it.

I paced as he read. Every so often, I walked over behind him to see where he was up to.

Leonard said. "Let me finish. Do you mind?"

"Sorry. Do you like it?"

"I'll tell you when I'm finished. Go make a drink, you're driving me batty."

From the bar, I said, "If you don't like it I think I'll jump off the Santa Monica pier."

I was always so dramatic.

Leonard read the last page of the script and said, "I think it plays."

"Really?" I said.

"Kind of."

"What do you mean 'kind of?'"

"Well, the dialogue in the first act is sort of weak, it needs some action in the second act and the denouement is so-so. But it plays."

"If the dialogue is weak in the first part, it needs more action in the second act and the denouement is—"

"It doesn't matter," said Leonard. "If you get a couple of stars no one will notice."

"That's some critique. It sounds like I wrote the side of a cereal box."

"But I think I can sell it."

"You think you can sell it?"

"I have a friend, well, an acquaintance, at Fox. She's a reader with a lot of clout and no taste. If I can get it to her maybe she'll recommend it."

"How do you know her?" I asked.

"I used to screw her."

"What would I do without you?"

"You'd probably starve," he said.

That afternoon, Leonard went off to meet his reader friend who worked at Fox. I was standing on the lawn, when he came home, three hours later.

"What?" I said, hopefully. "I see a big smile on your face. Tell me."

Leonard said, "Lester, Lester, Lester, Lester."

"A four-Lester message," I shrieked. "Say it."

"Do I have news for you," Leonard said.

"You didn't?"

"Yes, I did. I think I may have just gotten someone to option your screenplay."

"Option?"

"Lester, this is Hollywood. In this town nobody sells anything. They option."

"So how does a screen writer make any money?"

"Listen, do you know there are writers who live in Bel Air, in million dollar homes, who've never sold a script? Your screenplay is just lousy enough for somebody to option it."

"Who took an option on my script?" I asked.

"Peter Sellers' manager."

"You're putting me on. Peter Sellers? He's a comic genius!"

"He's sending it to him as we speak."

"Peter Sellers is—"

"Maybe, I said maybe, going to play the lead in your picture."

Suddenly, I noticed that there were some people gathering around us.

I said to them, "Can you believe it? Peter Sellers may star in my movie."

They all cheered.

A Japanese man, holding a rake (he was a gardener) said, "Make sure you get sole birring."

A woman pushing a baby carriage said, "Don't let the bastards off the hook on residuals."

A kid going by on a skateboard said, "Don't forget foreign rights." Everybody seemed to be in the movie business.

I said, "Leonard, I'm buying you the biggest dinner you can order at the Brown Derby."

Leonard said, "Don't you think we'd better wait until Peter Sellers reads it?"

How I Learned to Start Worrying and Hate Options

Peter Sellers' manager took a two-week option on the script. That is, he had two weeks to decide whether or not Peter Sellers would do the movie, and he said he'd get back to me. Meanwhile, I bought an old convertible Chevrolet and was driving it with the top down. I knew it was bad luck to buy the car before a deal was done, but I couldn't help it. I was certain Peter Sellers would love it. What film-goers saw as broad comedy was the result of incredible preparation, an exquisite sense of timing and sheer comic genius. I didn't care if the movie-goers understood how outstanding his talent was. I just knew that he was going to read my script, which was designed specifically for a comedian of his subtle yet hysterical interpretation.

Secretly, I hoped it wasn't too good to be true.

It was a glorious day. The sun was shining. I was probably among the happiest persons in the world. After all these months, I had a script optioned. For real money. It wasn't a lot but enough to make me feel wonderful. One of the biggest stars in the world was probably—well, possibly—going to star in my picture.

I was rolling down Rodeo Drive in a beatific fog, when a Rolls Royce pulled in front of me and cut me off. As I jammed on the brakes, from the Rolls came—I couldn't believe it—Jerry Lewis.

The Jerry Lewis.

"Lester Cooley?" he yelled.

"Colodny," I shouted back.

"You know who I am?"

"Of course. You're Jerry Lewis."

"The one. The only," Jerry said.

"How do you know me?" I asked.

"How do I know? I know everybody in this town."

People were beginning to surround us. A little boy approached Jerry. "Jerry, can I have your autograph?"

Jerry whipped out a pen and signed the kid's autograph book.

A woman pushed her way to the front of the rest and said, "Mr. Lewis, I saw your last picture and I loved it. I loved it and all your other pictures." Jerry Lewis kissed the woman and she ran over to another woman and shouted, "He kissed me. Here." She pointed to her nose. "Jerry Lewis kissed me, here."

Now there were about a hundred fans clamoring for his autograph. From his glove compartment, Jerry pulled out a pile of photographs and passed them out to the crowd.

"Now," Jerry said to the crowd with his hands empty, "no more, please. I have business to do."

The crowd started to disperse, but slowly. After all, it was Jerry Lewis.

He said to me, "Guess what? I'm coming to Fox."

I said, "That's great." What the heck was this all about? Why was he cutting me off to tell me he was going to Fox?

"They bought out my contract. From Paramount."

"I think that's swell," I said. I still couldn't fathom why Jerry Lewis was stopping me and talking to me like we were old friends.

"You don't get it, do you?" Jerry said.

"No. I'm sorry but—"

"I'm going to produce, direct and star in your script."

"You're doing my script?"

"They gave it to me last night."

"Who gave it to you?"

"The studio. Fox."

"What happened to Peter Sellers?"

"What has Peter Sellers got to do with it?"

"His manager took a two week option on it."

"That two-bit schlock artist," said Jerry. "No. I got it this morning. I read it. I loved it. Loved it, do you hear? So, this morning I told Paramount to go screw, I moved over to Fox, and tomorrow we're giving your script to my writers for a quick rewrite. Congratulations, pal." He shook my hand, got back in his Rolls, and pulled away.

A policeman rode up on a motorcycle. "You'll have to move that car, sir."

"He's doing my script," I said, in a daze.

"Who?"

"Jerry Lewis."

"Jerry Lewis? That was Jerry Lewis I just missed? How do you like that? I missed him by two seconds. Damn it. Did you say Jerry Lewis is going to star in a script you wrote?"

"Yes."

"Congratulations. That's fantastic."

To the crowd that was re-forming around us, he said, "Did you hear? Jerry Lewis is doing his script."

To me he said, "What did you say your name was?"

"I didn't say. But it's Colodny."

To the crowd the cop announced, as if it were the Academy Awards, "How do you like that. I just met Mr. Lewis's writer, Mr. Kooly."

They all applauded and cheered. He got off the cycle. He took my arm and walked me away from the crowd. "Mr. Kooly, you know I don't do this full time?"

I said, "Do what?"

He gestured at his uniform. "This."

"You don't?"

"Nah. It's only a gig to keep me going while I'm making rounds. I'm in the Screen Actors Guild," he said proudly.

I nodded. "I think I know what you mean," I said.

"Sig Froman is my screen name. My agent is Martin Cohen."

"I'll try to remember that," I said trying to edge myself away.

"You don't have to," he said and handed me a card. It read:

<blockquote>
Sig Froman
Character Actor
213-555-7890 or call
Jack Abelow.
</blockquote>

"Jack Abelow" had a pencil mark through it and in its place was written "Martin Cohen." The cop said, as I was starting up my car, "I just changed agents. That Abelow couldn't get me arrested."

I drove for a few blocks. Then I pulled over to the side, stopped, and put my head down on the steering wheel. "Jerry Lewis," I moaned. "And they told me Peter Sellers."

Sitting in Leonard's living room downing my fourth scotch I said, "Can you imagine? My first script. Sold. And who gets his dumb hands on it?"

Leonard said, "She told me it was going to Peter Sellers."

"Well, Jerry Lewis got it. By hand. Fox sent it to him. He read it and quit Paramount. They start rewriting the script today!"

"Who?"

"Jerry Lewis' writers, that's who."

"They'll mangle it," Leonard said.

"Tell me about it."

"Those writers are the wreckers of the industry."

"Why couldn't I rewrite it?" I moaned.

Leonard said, "Take the money and run. All the way to the bank."

So what, you might be thinking. Take the money and run. Get over yourself, Colodny.

But let me ask you this. Whoever you are, whatever you do, it's important that you're good at it, right? Parent, architect, long haul trucker, landscaper, small business owner, shipping magnate, it doesn't matter.

It really is about the quality of what we do and how we go about doing it. I had tried so hard and so long on behalf of others, and finally, here was my chance to do what I did best.

The intense feeling of rejection. Knowing not only that Peter Sellers was not reading my script but that Jerry Lewis was rewriting it for himself, made me feel dreadful. And I felt awful about it too. I had rewritten it, quickly, beautifully, with little flourishes and innuendos that were specifically designed for Peter Sellers' sensibilities and style.

Yes, Jerry Lewis was a star.

But, truthfully, there were few movies that Jerry Lewis made, even though they were great hits, that had anything redeeming about them. They were simply vehicles for him to mug, clown, and leer his way around the sets with his same old, same old interminable grimacing.

My vision of creating a picture with a little class went down the drain. I felt sick. All those days and nights, working, writing, rewriting, revising, honing, were a waste of time.

For days, I wandered around in my underwear. Unshaved. Unbathed. I was a depressed, disillusioned, despairing mess.

Leonard finally said to me, "Lester, you are cocking up my house."

"What?"

"You heard me. You are welcome to stay here forever. But you cannot, you must not, moon over a lost script. First of all, you got paid for it. No, wait, let me finish. You got paid for a job. That's all it was. A job. You are in Hollywood. Land of the narcissist, home of the depraved. Writers here are a dime a dozen. Nobody cares about writers. Or their words. All they care about is going to Chasen's and playing tennis and kissing one another's asses, on each cheek at cocktail parties, and telling each other how much they loved, make that adored, their last pictures. With their fingers crossed of course.

"Lester, listen to me. Nobody here gives a damn about anyone but themselves. It's survival of the fittest. That means you don't take anyone or yourself, especially yourself, that seriously. Seriously, trust me on this.

"You wanted to be a writer? So write and get over it already."

"What about integrity?" I asked.

Leonard looked at me in astonishment. "Integrity? Integrity? I love you," Leonard said. "You know that? You're the only guy I know who would have the *cajones* to use that word on this coast."

Dave Garroway being kissed by a chimp on *The Today Show.*

This is believed to be a unique image used to illustrate an event. Used under fair use laws.

Lester (on the left) playing miniature golf in Hawaii before leaving for The Philippines. (Left)

Lester with his shipmates trying to find the LST 23. Lester is the second from the right. (Below)

Lester performing at Tamiment in 1951.

This is believed to be a unique image used to illustrate an event. Used under fair use laws.

Lester (middle) at the 1960 Democratic National Convention in Los Angeles.

Lester (way far right) at Tamiment with Hilly Elkins (center), Larry Holofcener (lyricist, back row, third from left), Jerry Bock (composer for *Fiddler on the Roof*) and Herb Ross (Barbara Streisand's choreographer and director) right center, Herb Reich (grinning), Barbara Cook (left, with her back to the camera), and Edy (in the hat).

Lester with his Emmy Award for writing, producing and directing *The Baja Marimba Band*.

Paul McCartney (above) and John Lennon (below) with Roy Gerber, taken when The Beatles stayed in Los Angeles in 1964.

Roy with George Harrison (above) and Ringo Starr (below).
Personal photos used to illustrate a particular event under fair use laws.

A publicity shot of Lester. (Right)

Lester behind the camera.

Roy Gerber with William B. Williams (WNEW disc jockey). It was Williams who coined the moniker "Chairman of the Board" for Frank Sinatra.

Et tu, Lester? Lester poses in an ad for Xerox in his finest Toga.

Roy Gerber, Red Buttons, an unknown woman and Lester.

The title page of the playbill from *Fun City* with Joan Rivers.

This is a unique image used to illustrate an event. Used under fair use laws.

NATIONAL THEATRE
LOUIS A. LOTITO • • • • MANAGING DIRECTOR

ALEXANDER H. COHEN
and
ROCKY H. AOKI
present

JOAN RIVERS GABRIEL DELL
ROSE MARIE
in
FUN CITY
A New Comedy by
LESTER COLODNY   JOAN RIVERS   EDGAR ROSENBERG
with
VICTOR ARNOLD
LOUIS ZORICH   PIERRE EPSTEIN   HOWARD STORM
RENEE LIPPIN   J. J. BARRY

Special Guest Star
PAUL FORD
Directed by
JERRY ADLER

Scenery by   *Costumes by*   *Lighting by*
RALPH ALSWANG   ANN ROTH   JULES FISHER

Production Associate   *Associate Producer*
HILDY PARKS   ROY A. SOMLYO

Encore. Encore.

The good stuff.

Old Grand-Dad

KENTUCKY STRAIGHT BOURBON WHISKEYS, 86 PROOF AND 100 PROOF BOTTLED IN BOND. OLD GRAND-DAD DISTILLERY CO., FRANKFORT, KY. 40601.

Two Bachelors and Six Kids

When I moved out of Leonard's house Dee and the kids joined me. We tried to make it work, but the show business thing was a deal-breaker. She never recovered from the shock of our wedding which set the tone for everything that followed. She just didn't know what she was getting into. We stayed friendly so we could share the kids.

After we divorced, I ran into Roy Gerber, who was an agent at the Music Corporation of America. Roy was a fabulous agent. In fact, he was among those responsible for bringing the Beatles to America for their first performance.

We hit it off beautifully and he asked me if I would like to share a house with him.

(Before I go on, I have to tell you that Roy had three children and he had custody of them. I never knew why and I never asked him. It was none of my business.)

He had a huge house up on Coldwater Canyon in Los Angeles and had plenty of room for me. I told him that I had custody of my three children every weekend and all summer long but he shrugged it off.

"We have plenty of space. I have seven bedrooms," he said.

Roy's children were two boys and a girl just about the same age as mine were and they all got along famously. But one day the housekeeper, who kept the place sane, left for Haiti.

We were bereft. Two bachelors and six kids. This wasn't going to be pretty.

Now, though Roy's children were the same age as mine there were some profound differences. My kids were polite and sweet. Roy's were absolute hellions, as he cheerfully admitted to anybody who asked.

One day Roy answered an advertisement, in a local newspaper, that said there was a nanny for hire.

Roy said to me, "Lester, can I borrow your kids?"

"Borrow my kids? What for?"

"Well, when I interview this lady I'd like to introduce her to some, you know. . .mannerly children."

"Isn't that a little like the old bait and switch? Don't you think that's a little unfair?" I said.

"Nah," he said gesturing with his hand. "She'll be just like you. Once she gets used to my kids she'll love them."

So, that weekend, when my three came to visit me, I said to them, "Listen, I want you to go with Uncle Roy to meet someone. Just be quiet and be polite and don't say anything."

Kim Elizabeth was seven, Kathy Jill six and Mace Matthew was just three. And they went along with Roy because Uncle Roy was a hoot and they enjoyed every second with him.

Well, Roy went down to Alvarez Street, where the woman lived, and introduced himself and then said, "Oh, by the way, these are some of my children."

My kids were so well mannered and polite that when Roy told her about the house and where she would live and the salary she would get, she readily agreed to come to work for us. They shook hands and as they were leaving, my son Mace, who was three, tugged on Roy's sleeve.

"What is it?" Roy asked.

Mace said, in his most piercing little boy voice, "I have to go to the bathroom, Uncle Daddy."

The exchange escaped the woman and she came to live with us.

It was as Roy predicted. His kids were dreadful. Mine were delightful. She stayed with Roy for years.

Roy was a beautiful man. Not only was he tall and handsome, he had a great wit.

Everything, everything that came out of his mouth was dryly humorous and our six children loved him like the father and surrogate father that he was.

Roy and Irving

After I moved out of Leonard's, he had begun to collect more and more of Hollywood's losers and now that I was making a few bucks, I was no longer an eligible guest.

I met Roy Gerber at the Hollywood Bowl, a month before the Beatles took America by storm. We hit it off fabulously and he invited me to come live in his guest house.

Signed photographs of him with Paul McCartney and the other Beatles, Frank Sinatra, Johnny Carson, Sammy Davis Jr., Dihann Carroll, Dean Martin, Perry Como, Milton Berle, you name them, adorned the walls of his den, his living room, his bedroom, and his life.

Roy was the key, the connection, the brilliant uber-agent, who single-handedly booked just about every other luminary in the firmament that played the Las Vegas Strip.

And he not only persuaded the owners of the mammoth casinos to buy the mega stars at astronomical figures; once installed, he cared for and catered to them, cajoled them, listened to them, admonished them, criticized their acts, suggested changes in their material, the manner in which they presented themselves. He shared their secret qualms, uncertainties, and egocentric ambitions.

Roy was "the most incredible agent in the world."

And wide-eyed and awestruck, there I was, living and breathing among all those celebrities, whom I got to meet and enjoy, when I moved in with him.

How to explain Roy?

A Funny Thing Happened

He was very much the grownup in the entertainment world. But he was a giant kid who never forgot the importance of play and sheer joyfulness. That "kid" part included the ability to dance through life. Anyone who wanted to join in was invited.

Roy was also an inveterate, which is to say chronic, continuing and incurable collector. He was up to his eyebrows in memorabilia. Not just any memorabilia, mind you. It had to be authentic memorabilia.

His house was an amusement park. The garden included all kinds of colorful flowers and was planted with bowling balls, wire sculptures, loopy artifacts of every kind and innumerable signs.

One read, "Gluck's Hillside, Rooms Available."

All along Coldwater Canyon, in the fashionable section of Los Angeles, Roy had planted signs that read: "Three Miles to Gluck's Hillside," "Two Miles to Gluck's Hillside" and at the bottom of our hill, "Turn Here for Gluck's Hillside."

At the top of the hill there was a sign, "Gluck's Hillside, Breakfast, Lunch and Dinner Served."

Inside the house were pinball games, bowls of candy, golf clubs by the dozens and an enormous collection of hats of every size and shape, from every country on the planet.

Life at Roy's was one crazy-ass wonderful merry-go-round and everyone who stayed, visited or spent an afternoon there enjoyed the most fabulous times anyone could have.

Did I mention the birds?

Roy also had birds. Hundreds of them, in a giant aviary. It sounded like a veritable rainforest, with all the singing, murmuring, calling, cooing, clacking and chattering. They talked and gossiped and courted all day, and that melodious sound was punctuated with the whirring noise of tiny wing beats fluttering through the greenery.

Roy loved caring for those birds. He loved to feed them, talk to them and simply watch them.

But most of all, Roy loved Irving. Irving lived alone, in a separate tremendous black cage, with lots of room to move. Irving was Roy's pride and joy. His one and only mynah bird.

At night, when he came home to feed the bird, one could hear him talking to Irving and telling him about his day.

The thing was that mynah birds, like cockatoos and parrots, require a tremendous amount of interaction. They are terrifyingly smart. Which means leaving them alone in a cage, albeit a big one, was tantamount to caging a bright three-year-old.

Let me digress for a moment.

One day, my sister Della, who was a good friend of Roy's, came up to the house for lunch. She had been to our place (I was a semi-permanent guest) many times, enough to know that every time she came, some new crazy something would have been acquired or added since her last visit.

She got to the front gate and pushed a button on the head of a statue of Mickey Mouse. Up went the gate and she drove up, up, up the hill to our house.

(Oh, I forget to mention: the front lawn, landscaped with beautiful hedges and flowers, had, among the plants, a row of speakers from a defunct drive-in movie, several parking meters and a half dozen old street lampposts. And inside there were the collections of signed photographs I told you about and multitudinous posters of every TV and movie show Roy had ever seen, a dozen or so slot machines, a ski ball game, a snooker table, gumball machines, punchboards, ancient Coca Cola signs, more bowls of candy and more stuff than anyone could remember from one visit to the next).

As Roy and Della were about to have lunch, she happened to notice the huge aviary built onto the back wall of the house. It was at least ten feet high, fifteen feet long and about five feet deep. It was filled with parakeets.

"Roy," Della exclaimed, "how many birds do you have in there?"

"Two hundred."

"Wow! How many did you start with?" she asked.

"Four hundred."

That was Roy.

They sat down to lunch. It was then that Della glanced out the patio door and spotted the huge cage with the big black bird in it. The cage was sitting directly in the hot sunlight.

"Roy," she said, "why is the bird in that cage sitting in the hot sun? Why don't you take him inside?"

"Oh that bird? He's a mynah bird. Marlon gave him to me when he came back from Tahiti." (Marlon Brando was Roy's neighbor). "He won't die from a little sunlight."

"Roy," she said, "it's too hot out there."

"Nah, I'm not taking him inside. He's a pain in the ass. Talks all the time."

"He talks?"

"That's Irving. I taught him a few words and now he won't shut up."

"Roy, I insist that you take him inside," she said.

Roy made like he was annoyed. "Do you want that bird?" he said.

"Do I want the bird?"

"Yeah. Do you want him?"

"Yes," she answered, "I want the bird."

"Then take him."

"Take him?"

"You said you wanted him so take him."

"Just like that?"

"Just like that."

"What do you feed him?" she asked.

"Oh, canned fruit salad. Not too much. Get the generic with the light syrup. It's cheaper."

"Well I can't take him today," she said. "Will it be alright if I pick him up on Thursday?"

"Sure, anytime," said Roy.

So Della went home and told her kids they were getting a mynah bird that talked. They were absolutely thrilled.

The next afternoon, she and her four kids set out in an open convertible that she borrowed (the cage was enormous) to pick up the talking mynah bird. It was a lovely spring day and they arrived at the house in time for Roy to give the kids a tour. It was Roy's greatest enjoyment.

The children romped around for awhile, ate candy and ice cream and played the machines. Then Roy helped Della put the bird cage in the car and they were off for home.

Now, as my sister told me, as they drove toward home the kids kept trying to get the bird to talk.

"Irving want a cracker?"

Nothing.

"Hello, hellooo."

Nothing.

They tried whistling.

Nothing.

The kids kept trying but the bird wasn't talking. The children were hugely disappointed.

The route home was on Coldwater Canyon, a road that separates the Valley (where Della lived) from Beverly Hills and Los Angeles (where Roy's house was located).

At the top was a four-way stop where only one car passed at a time. It was close to rush hour, so the cars were backed up quite a way. Theirs was the next car to cross the road, when the bird opened its beak and in a booming voice screamed out, "Move that fucking car, you putz! Get that motherfucker out of the way! Kiss my ass, you shitheel! You're an asshole!" and other delightful epithets.

It was unreal.

People were stopping their cars and getting out to see where these obscenities were coming from. Luckily the car in front of Della's had gone through the intersection and she roared off before her car could be identified as the source of all the profanity.

Now the kids were excited. Not only did the mynah bird talk, he had some serious shit to say. They were hysterically falling over each other as this nutty bird continued its verbal tirade all the way home.

Although he eventually became one of the family and calmed down (because Roy was not there to reinforce his behavior), Della did keep him away from friends and neighbors, whom he seemed to delight in shocking.

Well, a week passed and Roy called Della to complain. He was indignant. "I had that bird for a long time. Not only did he not say goodbye, according to your kids, he doesn't even miss me!"

As it happens, my sister is and was as nutty as Roy so she bought some sandpaper cage liner and with a fine, scratchy, pointed pen she wrote the following letter to Roy:

>Dear Roy,
>
>Sorry I didn't get a chance to say goodbye.
>This nice lady with the beautiful kids picked me up (out of the sun) and took me in an open car to a beautiful house.
>I have my own room. They call it the den.
>I stay inside (they have central air conditioning).
>They feed me lots of fruit salad. Del Monte to be specific. With heavy syrup.
>In short, schmuck, who needs you.
>Go fuck yourself.
>
>Irving,
>
>The Bird.

The Beatles are Coming - 1964

Roy was not only fun and silly, but when he scored, he always shared.

He and his partner, Norman Weiss, (both of whom worked for MCA, the giant talent agency) had managed to bring the Beatles to the Hollywood Bowl for their first American appearance in the west. This was a history making moment in my kid's lives. Everyone was agog.

The Beatles were coming. The Beatles were coming! Screams, hysteria, excitement.

And my kids and Roy's were going to get to see them.

They couldn't wait to go to school for the next few days. Every kid in America had heard about the Beatles' appearance. And when our kids told their friends that they were going to the Hollywood Bowl, they were the envy of their schools.

They all primped and posed and wondered what it would be like.

Even at their young ages (the oldest was nine, the youngest was six) their excitement was unbelievable.

Then came the big night. Roy arranged for a long limo and we drove to the Bowl—six children, Roy and me. And when the guards let us in and we drove up to a special entrance I thought my little ones would die on the spot.

Now before we entered the Bowl, I said to my children and Roy's, "I don't want any screaming. Get it?" They nodded. We were led through a special door and up to our box. . .in the center of the Hollywood Bowl!

The kids dashed into the arena.

As soon as we entered the box they, along with a half a jillion other kids, started to scream. The concert wasn't to begin for another half hour. I'd never seen or heard anything like it.

Then the Beatles appeared. The four long-haired, skinny kids began to sing. I don't know how anyone heard them. In fact, as I was later to find out no one could. They couldn't even hear themselves playing. They were accompanied by an hour and a half of ear-piercing shouting, yelling, dancing and fainting.

The extraordinary cacophony began to drop in decibels when the Beatles finally left the stage.

I had been saving this one. I turned to the kids and yelled over the moaning and sobbing crowd, "How would you like to meet the Beatles?" They looked at me with open-mouthed awe.

The next thing we knew, we were being led down to our limo and then off to a huge mansion in Beverly Hills where the Beatles' manager had ensconced them for three nights.

The place was complete bedlam when we entered. Girls and women of all ages running around. "Did you see them? Has anyone seen them?"

A half-clad woman of thirty-five or so came rushing out of a bedroom. "I just fucked a Beatle!" she screeched and ran out to her car.

Three girls of indeterminate age came out of a bedroom and squealed, "We just—did them!" And ran out to their waiting cars so they could get home quickly to tell their friends that they had just indulged in fellatio with a Beatle.

Roy and I exchanged panicked looks. Then we looked at our six children. They were confused. Roy motioned with his head. "Let's get the hell out of here."

Just then Paul McCartney came out.

Thank God, I thought to myself. He was wearing clothes.

He came over to our children and Roy introduced them one by one. And Paul took a magic marker and signed his name on all our kids' clothes and hats. They were ecstatic.

That night as I tucked them into bed, my daughter Elizabeth whispered, "Daddy, I know it was bad, 'cause I saw your face, but what does 'I just fucked a Beatle' mean?"

I leaned down, kissed her goodnight and said, "It's how people without good manners like yours, say how much she appreciated their singing."

Life with Danny Simon

At some point, Roy and I acquired a third roommate. We'd both known him for years. He was a brilliant comedy writer, the brother of Neil Simon and an enormous noodge, Danny Simon.

He was one of those creatures that push-overs like Roy and me were always taking pity on. After his divorce, Danny had nowhere to go. Nowhere to live. So we took him in and the three of us, all bachelors, lived together for about six months.

And that half-year was a calamity, to say the least.

Danny wasn't simply obsessive-compulsive, he was a maniac. He cleaned incessantly. No matter where you sat, the moment you got up, Danny sneaked in and fluffed the pillows. Sometimes before both cheeks had cleared the chair.

No matter where you smoked (Roy and I smoked in those days) Danny was dogging our heels, holding out an ashtray. The guy was certifiably nuts.

We couldn't deal with it but we had to take care of him because nobody else would.

A holy war was declared on crumbs in the kitchen. God forbid you should leave a newspaper on a chair to get up and get a drink. It wouldn't be there when you got back.

Socks and other clothes were forbidden to have contact with any furniture, floor, chair, counter or couch. Underwear left anywhere was a mortal sin and went right into the garbage.

Danny did all the cooking so if you weren't there on time, you didn't eat.

For a few weeks it was funny. Roy and I laughed. It was just Danny's way of working out his frustration with his ex-wife. But it didn't stop. The madness dragged into a month, then two months, and we realized that it wasn't so much funny-crazy, as crazy-crazy.

At the four and a half month mark, we were both stark, raving, mad.

Finally, Roy said to me, "We have to do something about this insanity."

"You invited him to stay here. It's your house. Do something. Say something," I said.

"What should I say?" pleaded Roy.

"Tell him that. . .if he doesn't stop this. . .this. . .Tell him he must cease being our mothers," I whimpered.

"I'm going to tell him that?"

"Yes. Because if you won't then I will," I stated. "Then I'll kill him."

"Fine. I'll do it. You'd yell and upset him," said Roy.

"All right. You tell him."

"Okay, I will. Now how do I start?"

"Chicken shit," I said.

"Horse manure," was Roy's response.

We walked into the living room where Danny, in an apron, was vacuuming the rug for the third time that morning.

"Danny," Roy began.

"Watch your feet," Danny yelled.

"Danny," Roy repeated.

"How many times do I have to tell you both to wipe your shoes off before you walk on my clean floors?" Danny yelled.

"Danny, Roy has something to tell you," I said.

But Danny wasn't listening. He was engaged in picking up a tiny piece of lint the vacuum had refused to suck up. Roy and I exchanged helpless shrugs. We went into the kitchen and pulled two bottles of beer out of the refrigerator.

"Use coasters," I said. "We don't want to leave spots on the table."

The Blind Date

After Dee divorced me, I became a permanent house guest of Roy Gerber.

One night, Roy got out of his car and said, "What do you have on for tonight?"

"Nothing," I said.

"How would you like a date for tonight?"

"A what?"

"A date. Pick her up at Eight Vista Lane, in Brentwood, at seven. It's all set. You'll love her."

"I don't have a car," I said.

"Take mine, I'm not going anywhere."

"What's her name?"

"Lana."

Dammit. Now I had to shave and shower. What the hell. It was better than sitting home watching television.

I drove to Eight Vista Lane, Brentwood. It was a private home. Three stories high. Wow, what a place to live. I rang the doorbell and a maid came to the door.

"She'll be ready in two minutes," she said sweetly and left me in the parlor.

I wandered around the front room looking at the decor. The living room was covered with pictures. Frank Sinatra, Cary Grant, James Mason. Boy, I thought, she must really be star-struck.

Then she came down the stairs and I nearly fell over. It was. . .it was. . .

Lana Turner!

I had a date with Lana Turner? That son-of-a-bitch, Roy! He knew it would floor me. I was so dumbstruck, I could hardly utter a word.

My whole body broke a sweat. My elbows were perspiring. My eyebrows were wet. I knew my pupils had dilated like those of a cartoon wolf's, but I managed a covert deep breath as I said, "Good evening, Miss Turner, I'm Lester Colodny."

Awkwardly, I stuck my hand out to shake, but she grabbed my arm, pulled me close, and said, in that deep Lana Turner voice, "Let's go, Lester. We'll talk in the car."

Ten minutes later we were on our way to Malibu. As we were driving, I said to her, "I have to tell you, Miss Turner—"

She said, "Miss Turner? No, no, no. It's Lana."

Now I knew that she knew that she was the center of the Hollywood solar system and I was a mere planet, circling in thrall to her gravitational power. Yet she let it be known from the git-go, she wanted to be just Lana. Lana and Lester. Lester and Lana. That's all. Two human beings, a nice night, on our way to a nice party.

To help me feel at ease, she cozied up to me and said, "Tell me all about you. What do you do? Are you an actor?"

"No, I'm a writer. And I was a producer of *The Today Show*."

"On TV, with Dave Garroway?" she said, as if it were the greatest show on earth. "I watched it all the time. I still do. That is, when I get up that early."

"Really?" I said. "Did you see the show with the monkeys?"

"The monkeys?" This time it was her pupils that dilated. "I can't believe it! My God, they were all over Florence Henderson!" And she roared with laughter.

Suddenly, I felt like I knew her. Like we were old friends.

I said, "I've seen all your movies. You are such a gifted actress."

"I appreciate that coming from a show business person," she said.

"I'll never forget the way you played Cora in *The Postman Rings Twice*," I said.

She batted her eyes at me.

Then I said, "Lana, I have to tell you. I have had your picture on my wall since—"

She said, "How sweet. I was your pinup girl?" She said, "You know, I like you, Lester."

I couldn't utter a sound. I was staggered. Lester and Lana Turner. It had a certain ring to it.

Suddenly, the ghost of Johnny Stompanado was banging on the door of my subconscious.

You're kidding. You don't know who he is? Let me save you the Google search.

Rough early life, joined the Marines, saw action in WWII, came home to Illinois, dumped his wife and child and headed for Hollywood. Hit the big time as a small-time gangster. A charming, well-connected, abusive, possessive and probably pathologically jealous jerk who had a torrid and tempestuous affair with Lana Turner.

In 1958, her fourteen-year-old-daughter killed him. With a kitchen knife. In defense of her mother.

Now, Johnny still had friends. Big, ugly, very mean guys who knew how to carry a grudge. What if they had a directive from Johnny's grave to avenge him by doing damage to any guy who got within ten feet of Lana? I know it sounds melodramatic but this was Hollywood, you know. I tried to look casual as I scanned the rear window, watching for headlights.

I peeked over at her. She was a few years older than me but she still looked terrific. The quintessential "Sweater Girl" whose discovery at Schwab's Drug Store created the iconic legend of Hollywood. The drop-dead beauty who was married eight times. Who reputedly had affairs with every leading man in Hollywood including Clark Gable, Victor Mature, Robert Taylor, Fernando Lamas, and even Mickey Rooney.

We got to the party and walked in. If you think I was stunned by the appearance of Lana Turner as my date, you'll understand that I was in an altered state when I looked around the room.

There, drinking and smoking and talking were—are you ready? Cary Grant, Eva Marie Saint, James Mason, Lee Marvin (who had just finished making *Cat Ballou*), Ernest Borgnine, Lucille Ball, Harry Guardino, and Mel Shavelson, the director. They all made obeisance to Lana as if she were Mary Magdalene.

"Lana darling, how are you? And who is this perfectly lovely boy with you?"

"Lana, would you like a drink?"

A Funny Thing Happened

"Lannie, we saw your last picture, you were ravishing."

It was a party thrown by Claire Bloom and Rod Steiger, her current husband, who was a notoriously good actor and an even more infamous brawler.

Lana introduced me to everyone. "This is Lester Colodny; he produced Dave Garroway's show, on NBC."

Unaccountably, everyone wanted to know all about Dave Garroway. I was in heaven. The star of the party. I had stories to tell. Naughty and narcissistic doings to reveal.

And when I told them about the monkeys they screamed.

About eleven thirty, we had eaten and were having coffee when the fight started.

Rod Steiger and Lee Marvin, (another infamous tough guy), were brawling from one end of the house to the other. Two big, fairly brawny guys duking it out in old-style Western fashion. But this was for real. It began in the hall, progressed into the living room where furniture was flying as they battled, and everybody else scrambled to get out of the way. Those not directly in harm's way toasted and cheered on the action. I think Cary Grant was taking bets.

Steiger and Marvin had each other in a bear lock. They were trying to fling each other over a couch. Instead, they fell through a window (I know it sounds unbelievable, but I swear to you it happened) and into the pool. They were both so smashed that they didn't even know what they were fighting about. We pulled them apart, everyone accepted apologies and we went home.

On the way back, Lana said to me, "I'm so sorry, Lester. I didn't mean to take you to a brawl."

"No, no," I protested. "It was great."

We were nearing her house. I wanted desperately to ask her out again but I was tongue-tied. Why would she want to see me again? Well, she had told me she liked me. She had been very proud when all those stars crowded around me and asked me questions.

By the time we drove up to her house it was after midnight. And she kissed me. Not a passionate kiss. More like a friendly kiss. But she kissed me. Could she actually be attracted to me? Or was she just being friendly?

"Lester," she said, "I had the most marvelous evening."

She got out of the car and went into the house.

I drove home thinking, did she, was she? No, I decided, it was just a night out for her.

I stopped the car and walked over to a pay phone. I called the house. Roy answered. "You son of a bitch, Roy. Why didn't you tell me I would be going out with Lana Turner?"

He said, "I figured maybe one of Johnny's old crowd would take care of you and I could use your bedroom for another den."

A Funny Thing Happened

The Baja Marimba Band

From the telescript of an NBC TV special, "Jack Benny and the Baja Marimba Band," (that I wrote, directed and produced because no one else was available or would work for so little money).

>CLOSE UP on
>
>Jack Benny seated ringside.
>
>CUT TO
>
>Benny's POV (Point of View)
>
>The Baja Marimba band.
>
>(They are playing the last sixteen bars of their theme song.)
>
>CUT TO
>
>Jack Benny applauding.
>
>CUT TO
>
>The band bowing.
>
>CUT TO
>
>WIDE SHOT
>
>A waitress approaches Jack, surrounded by the band members. She puts a restaurant check in front of him.
>
>CUT TO
>
>MCU (Medium Close Up)
>
>Jack, as he picks up the bill and scans it.
>
>He flinches.

He does an excruciatingly funny take. (We are aware of how astronomical he thinks the check is.)

CUT TO

WIDER SHOT

Featuring the waitress who gives Jack an impatient look. (Looking resentfully)

Jack pulls a stocking purse from his jacket.

He counts out large bills.

CUT TO

TIGHT SHOT JACK

He is clearly in great psychic pain.

ANOTHER ANGLE

Featuring Jack.

He begins to get up.

The waitress stands there. (With hands on hips. She is waiting for her tip.)

CUT TO ANOTHER ANGLE

As Jack looks at her.

A BEAT.

Jack looks in the stocking purse.

A BEAT.

Jack looks back at her with a pathetic expression.

A BEAT.

Jack reaches into the purse and pulls out a coin.

He drops the coin on her tray.

SFX (Sound effect)

A clinking sound.

MEDIUM SHOT

Jack walks away as the Waitress, (pained) examines the coin with disdain.

The Emmy Award

I received a letter from the Academy of Television Arts and Sciences. It told me that I was a nominee in the categories of producer/director/writer of a ninety minute musical comedy special.

With Leonard in tow as my date, I made my way to the auditorium where an usher led us to our seats. We were seated down front.

I said to Leonard, "Is it possible?"

Thirty seven minutes later, Dick Van Dyke announced:

"The winner of best writer, director and producer, of a musical comedy special is (there is a chord played by the orchestra). . .for Jack Benny and the Baja Marimba Band."

I heard a tiny smattering of applause.

Leonard said, "Lester, it's you."

I managed to somehow get on my feet and stumbled to the stage. Dick Van Dyke had left but a beautiful girl handed me my EMMY.

I had won and I started to thank Jack Benny, the Baja Marimba band and the entire crew, but my throat seized up. Finally, I croaked, "I'd like to thank—"

The studio orchestra cut me off. They went to a commercial.

Another girl ushered me off the stage.

All around me, stars, producers, directors, writers, PR men, rushed up to one another, congratulating, kissing, hugging.

I stood alone, backstage at the Pantages Theatre, with an ersatz gold statue in my hand and a stab in my heart.

A Funny Thing Happened

I was a winner. The best producer, director, writer of a ninety-minute television musical comedy.

But no one knew my name. Except Kim, Kathy, Mace, and Dee.

The Night Belongs to Charlie

I finally sold a screen play. It was an original called *The Night Belongs to Charlie*, and was reported on the first page of the trade papers, the Hollywood Reporter and Variety:

> **Abby Acquires Colodny Script**
>
> Abby Productions Inc. has bought an original screenplay, *The Night Belongs to Charlie*, from screenwriter Lester Colodny according to Larry Price, Producer. Production is planned for early December in Bangkok, Hong Kong and Los Angeles.

Roy, Leonard and I were all wild with excitement. And Roy decided that it was time for a party. That night, as we were toasting my good fortune, the doorbell buzzer sounded.

Roy answered the door. It was two Los Angeles police officers.

"We had a report from one of your neighbors that you were tearing up the neighborhood," said the cop.

"No, sir," said Roy, "We were just tearing up some old IOUs, some bank demands for payment, some electric bills and some car payment demands."

"Are you telling me that's what we drove all the way up here for?"

"Sorry for the false alarm, gentlemen. Let us make it up to you," said Roy. He smacked his hands together, rubbing them in anticipation. "Now, who would like a drink?"

One cop looked at the other. "We go off duty in an hour," he whispered. "So why not call in and just say we have a collar?"

"Good thinking," said the first cop as he doffed his coat and proceeded to swill a tall vodka and orange juice, proffered by Leonard.

Ten minutes later, we were standing around the piano in the living room, singing our hearts out as Leonard played, when the buzzer at the front door sounded.

Roy answered the door again.

A disheveled and unkempt but very attractive Jimmy Boyd was leaning against the door jamb, blinking his eyes. (In case you don't remember Jimmy, he was famous for recording "I Saw Mommy Kissing Santa Claus.") He had been staying at Marlon Brando's house next door and had been wakened by the police siren. He wondered what was going on.

Suddenly, Jimmy spied the two L.A. policemen. "Kelly, what are you doing here?"

"We're investigating a report of loud behavior, Mr. Boyd," said the cop.

"It doesn't look like you're doing much investigating."

"You drink boiler makers, as I recall," said Officer Kelly.

The front door buzzer sounded again. Roy answered the door. Standing in the doorway was a very attractive young lady.

Roy shouted, "Dihann Carroll. When did you get back?" He ushered her in and shut the door.

"About ten minutes ago. I saw the lights on here and knew there was a party going on. By the way," she said, "Guess who you just slammed the door on?"

Roy ran to open the door again. There, with sheepish grins on their faces, were Lucille Ball and her husband, Desi Arnez, who said, "What are we, chopped liver?"

I couldn't believe my eyes and ears. Luci and Desi, Jimmy Boyd, and Dihann Carroll?

The party was beginning to take on an aura of a pre-celebration for the Academy Awards. It was great.

The doorbell rang again. I answered. It was the actor James Caan and two lovelies.

"We heard the patrol car and came over to see what happened."

Roy insisted they come in and join the party.

Leonard handed each one of them a glass of champagne and Lucy and I (Lucy and I, it was unbelievable) went into the kitchen and started scrambling in cupboards and the fridge for all the cheese and crackers we could find.

Lucille Ball!

Cheese and crackers!

And before you could say "Jackie Robinson," Jackie Robinson, the baseball player, and his lovely wife came by. He carried in a case of beer and his wife had the remnants of a turkey that they had had for dinner.

This was followed by a pizza man who delivered twelve pies and instead of a tip accepted autographs from everyone, including the cops.

The stereo was blasting, everyone was dancing, everybody was drinking and telling Roy what a wonderful host he was. The party was gaining momentum.

"What's the party for?" yelled someone through the screen door.

It was Sammy Davis Jr.

Sammy Davis Jr?

"What kind of schmuck are you?" sang Leonard as he played "What Kind of Fool Am I" and Sammy came in and lit up a stogie.

"Lester sold a screenplay," shouted Leonard.

"Who's Lester?" Sammy hollered above the noise.

"Me," I bellowed.

He lit up another stogie for me.

Then Dihann said, "I think we should toast all the great guys in the police department who keep this city safe from loud parties."

Everyone toasted.

Roy howled, "How about the neighborly concern of complete strangers?"

"Who's a stranger?" said Jimmy Caan. "How about toasting Lester putting us all in his new movie?"

Everyone rushed to the bar for refills. It was a mad, wonderful celebration.

If the doorbell rang, I certainly didn't hear it over the ruckus, but the next thing I knew, the front door flew open and Johnny Carson showed up.

Johnny Carson?

Sammy Davis and Lucy and Desi?

Dihann Carroll and Jimmy Boyd?

And they were toasting me, a world famous, anonymous writer.

I had to pinch myself. The ignominy of the EMMY award disappeared. I was, literally, the toast of the town.

Now, the party got wildly exuberant, as Johnny, with a drink in his hand, told stories. There was nobody in the world who could tell a story like Johnny.

Johnny Carshon. Me and Johnny Carshon and Lushi. I was getting a little tipshy.

As I frantically poked in a drawer for my EMMY, there was a huge cheer from outside the house. Everyone rushed to the windows and doors. There in the pool were Roy and one of our neighbors, a six-foot-five redhead, splashing at one another.

They were naked as jaybirds.

Someone yelled, "Hey, wait for me," stripped, grabbed a Donald Duck float ring, jammed it over his head and jumped in to the pool.

It was the beginning of bedlam. Now the rest of the neighborhood started coming over. Through the hedges. From between the trees. Up and down the road.

Before we knew it, the party had swelled to more than fifty and was growing by leaps and bounds.

Marlon Brando, who lived next door to Roy, showed up with three bottles of saki, and Mel Torme, who lived three doors down from Roy, poked his head in and asked if he could join the party.

It had become a grand bacchanalia.

I looked around, half drunk. Someone, I don't remember who, was shaking my hand, patting me on the back, asking me to tell him the story of the picture I had just sold.

I'd never been so elated in my life.

And all these unbelievable people to share it with. Everyone seemed genuinely happy for me.

They didn't know who I was, only that someone new had broken the invisible barrier of Hollywood.

I couldn't stop smiling. My cheeks were cramping from the Cheshire Cat grin wrapped twice around my face.

At four that morning, the last of our guests stumbled out of the house and down the road. It was quiet. The house looked like fairgrounds after a festival. There was wall to wall litter, but Roy, Leonard and I were a very sleepy but happy and triumphant threesome.

That afternoon, with a hangover the size of Texas, I drove into town to sign the contract at Larry Price's Abbey Productions.

The Abby office was empty except for a secretary.

I asked for Mr. Price.

She said, "Oh, Mr. Price left for Bali last night."

My stomach lurched violently.

"Left for Bali?" I said. "For Bali? I have a contract to be signed."

"Are you Colodny, the author of *The Night Belongs to Charlie*?" she asked.

"Yes."

"Mr. Price left me a note for you," she said.

The relief washing over me made me dizzy. It was alright. He left me a note. All was well.

She handed me the note. I read:

> "Dear Lester,
>
> Sorry about *Charlie*. We ran out of money. Maybe you can sell it to somebody else.
>
> Best Regards,
>
> Larry."

I started to fall into a chair when two men entered and started to remove the furniture.

The secretary was leaving. I pleaded with her, "That's it?"

She said, "Yep. That's the story."

I sat back in shock.

But one of the men came in and tapped me on the shoulder.

He gestured for me to get up.

Then he took the chair.

Have Gene, Will Travel

After being employed by Universal Studios, creating and producing a series for a whole season like *Tom, Dick and Mary*, (part of the three-series block called *Ninety Bristol Court*) and creating *The Munsters*, an enormous hit series, I was bereft.

Every series had an executive producer, so I would go around from studio to studio, like so many of the writers, hoping I could get assignments from them to write episodes for the many television shows. I reckoned that I had earned my stripes and that they would be fighting for my services.

But I discovered, to my dismay, that for every show there were a hundred others, producers and writers, many of them top guns, writing ideas, outlines, and synopses, on spec (speculation) in the hopes of getting a job fighting off the banks.

Here and there a producer took pity on me and I wrote segments for *Get Smart*, *Love American Style*, a whole season of *Doodletown Piper* shows and even cartoons like *Beetle Bailey*.

The pay was dreadful and the rewrites by the head writers of the programs made me feel like an amateur.

To my friends and family, I was in show business but in actuality, I was little more than a day worker.

Then one day, someone told me I could make some money writing special material for stars that were playing Las Vegas. I gassed up my convertible and made the trek through the desert to Sin City. Nobody knew from one shots and unemployment. They only knew I had been a big shot at Universal.

My first assignment was for a revue at the old Stardust Hotel and Casino where I wrote and directed the sketches for a corny revue that ran for nine months. And that drew the important entertainers to spice up their acts with jokes and comedy bits.

And despite my abhorrence for staging and writing for inflated egos, I was hired (I undertook assignments for) Joan Rivers and Dinah Shore.

Life in Los Angeles, in Hollywood, was, at best, tolerable. That is, if you were working. Especially at your usual trade. But every once in a while things became a little more bearable once I started getting paid for the special material assignments.

Writing special material was lucrative but harrowing. It was an experience that few writers ever attempted. That was because the writer had to tailor the material for the entertainer they were writing for. And writing for any star performing in Vegas was doubly dangerous.

First and foremost, the act was live. The material had to hold up to all kinds of audiences in all kinds of moods. Unlike Broadway, it was often very close-up live, and even if you had back-up dancers or whatever joining for a number or two, the star still had to carry the show. All by their lonesome.

Second, Vegas was the place that could make or break an individual entertainer's career in a heartbeat. Which meant that every word, every hand movement, body gesture, pause, nuance, line and song had to be dead on.

Does that mean that each entertainer (male or female) knew and understood what kind of material was right for them? What would be appropriate for the times? What they could pull off?

No, no, and no. And here is why. If a performer is a quality, professional talent, they have to—repeat, have to—be so involved in the doing that they are not aware of how it is appearing.

Otherwise they are outside the performance and every member of the audience knows it. As I said before, audiences are smart. And they're rarely wrong. So that's what writers, producers and directors are for. The good ones adapt their style to what each performer needs and is capable of delivering.

Does that mean the performer will go there?

No.

You see the movie equivalent of that reticence in all the ridiculous Hollywood sequels, from *Blast Them To Smithereens 2*, to *Return to Blast Them To Eternity 2*.

People are scared silly of new.

Originality can be dangerous. It can be possible poison at the box office.

One day, Eddie Sherman, an actor's rep whom everyone adored, called me and asked me if I would like to write a whole new Las Vegas act for Gene Barry.

Remember Gene? He was the television star of a hit show, *Have Gun Will Travel*, and was a sought-after act in Vegas because he was a triple threat, an actor who could also sing, dance and tell jokes. Sort of like an old-time Hugh Jackman.

But Gene had been using the same act for three years and now he needed a new presentation.

I called my friend, Ed Haas, and asked him if he would like to write an act.

"Sure thing," Ed replied, recognizing the signs. "I'm out of work too."

We worked feverishly for weeks, writing the act, searching out songs that would be apropos, thinking up bits of comedy. We hired a six-piece singing and dancing act to work behind Gene to give him some backing, and finished the act.

You know what? It looked great. Honest.

We performed it for Gene Barry's agents. They loved it. With the official seal of approval, it was finally time to perform it for Gene himself. When we finished, Gene said, "I don't know."

My heart began to pound.

"What don't you know about?" I asked.

"I'm not so sure about the songs and the comedy and the group. I don't know."

We had two weeks to rehearse the act. There was no time for rewriting. Gene was to open at the Riviera for two weeks at fifty thousand dollars a week. He was still very resistant to any changes from what he'd been doing. Then Eddie Sherman had a light-bulb moment.

He hired the orchestra at a prestigious downtown hotel during the afternoon. He asked me if I would perform the act, from start to finish, as Gene Barry. For Gene.

It was crazy. It was expensive. But we had to do something to prove to Gene that the act was a winner.

That Saturday afternoon, while the waiters and busboys were setting up the tables for the evening, the band, all sixteen of them, came in, looked over the arrangements, put them in order and said "Let's do it."

They were professionals. These guys could play any act off the cuff. Sight unseen.

I was dressed in a hired tuxedo, hat, gloves and cane, prepared to become Gene Barry for an afternoon.

I was incredibly nervous about performing, but I knew that material inside out. I helped create it. The songs, the patter and the moves with the group—I knew what I was doing. The orchestra played an intro chord, Eddie Sherman made the introduction.

The band launched into the opening of the first number, I strode onstage and sang my heart out.

For an hour and a half, I sang, clowned, moved, danced and went off to a rousing final number that would have made any crowd cheer.

Standing in the wings, I heard applause.

I peeked out.

All the waiters, the busboys and busgirls, the employees of the restaurant and hotel were cheering. The orchestra was standing with the violinists tapping their bows. A very rare occurrence.

The act was a hit. In fact, it was a smash.

For a few moments, it was as if I had opened at the Riviera myself in Las Vegas. I was higher than a kite. I walked over to Gene Barry and said, "Well Gene, there's your act. Tell me. Is it or isn't it a killer?"

Gene said, "It was killer. It was sensational. But that was you, Lester. What about me?"

That next week, Gene Barry opened at the Riviera in Las Vegas and performed his old act. And it was a very, very long time before I ever wrote special material again.

Hugh and the Bunnies

I was not only out of work, I was about to be out of a car. I took it to the carwash the day my lease was up. I was sitting there morosely contemplating my shoes when a man sat down next to me.

He said, "Excuse me, but aren't you Lester Colodny?"

"I think so," I answered.

He held out his hand. "I don't know if you remember me. My name is David Sontag."

"No, I'm sorry but the name doesn't ring a bell."

He said, "A few years ago, you were one of the producers of *The Today Show* with Dave Garroway. And I was a page at NBC, showing people around the studios."

"Really," I said. I wasn't listening to him very closely, I was thinking about how I would get back home after I returned the car.

He continued, "You were so nice to me in those days. You always showed me how *The Today Show* ran. You explained how the program was planned. You even introduced me to some of the stars. What are you doing now?"

I said, "As soon as I get my car washed, I'm going to drive it back to the rental place and then I'm probably going to walk in front of a bus."

"You're kidding," he said.

"Only partially. Truthfully, I have nothing on my plate. In fact, I don't even have a plate."

As our cars came out of the washing apparatus, he said, "I would like you to follow me."

"Follow you?"

"Yes." He got in his car and I trailed behind. We pulled up to a building on Wilshire Boulevard and got out.

"This way," he said.

I didn't even ask. I followed him up the stairs into a huge room, filled with bustling people.

"Everyone," he shouted. "Everyone, please gather round."

They assembled, about thirty or forty men and women.

He addressed them. "I want you to meet the new producer of *Playboy After Dark*, Lester Colodny. He's a dandy and I promise you'll love him."

I couldn't believe it. I was the new producer of the hour long, syndicated weekly production of a television program, starring that international maven of sex, Hugh Hefner.

Everyone applauded. They surrounded me, congratulated me and showed me to my corner office.

In the office I said to David Sontag, "I don't understand."

"Well, our producer was fired yesterday and I can't think of a better person to produce our show than you. I figured if I made it official with an announcement, you couldn't say no."

The show, as I said, was syndicated and broadcast over a hundred and five stations, at different times. So the themes, the guests and the jokes had to be timeless.

The girls, the models, were breathtaking (and for the most part rather dumb). All they had to do was wait for me to arrange them around the setting, which was an improvised sunken living room.

Before every show, I had the job of picking the most stunning females so that they adorned the inane chatter of Hugh Hefner and his guests.

Hefner sat, with his pipe in his mouth, and read from cue cards. Badly.

But his guests were the biggest stars. Bob Newhart, Sammy Davis Jr., Meredith MacRae, Roman Polanski, Otto Preminger, Dean Martin, Steve Allen, Ava Gardner, Michael Caine. You name the star, they were there.

Big name rock bands like The Grateful Dead, Steppenwolf, Three Dog Night, and The Nitty Gritty Dirt Band showed up in Hef's living room. And of course, the big name comedians, from George Carlin to George Burns, Joe E. Lewis to Jerry Lewis. It was a cornucopia of magnificent talent overseen by the dullest, dreariest, most colorless host, but it was a hit because of the guests.

I produced that show for two seasons. I do not know how I got through it. I have blocked most of it out of my mind. It was all a huge yawn.

The host was boring. The hostess, Barbie Benton, was even more boring. The writers were listless. The director was a drunk. David Sontag was nowhere to be found.

The guests appeared because they needed TV exposure and there was nowhere else except *The Johnny Carson Show* and an occasional variety program to get it.

Hefner had achieved worldwide fame with his magazine and a

mansion that hosted unbelievable parties. He had cultivated a reputation for being a swinger. His 727 flew around the world carrying the biggest personalities.

And yet he was dull. Duller. Dullest.

One day on the set I sent for him. It was time for him to introduce an act. There was no Hugh Hefner.

Finally, I went back to his dressing room myself and knocked on the door.

"Yes?" he answered.

I said, "Hef, they're waiting for you to introduce—"

He said, through the door, "I'm busy. I'm very busy. They'll have to wait."

Ten minutes later, he appeared, tucking in his shirt, his face covered with lipstick.

The swinger smirked at everybody on the set. Every one smiled back. They knew what he had been up to.

Barbie Benton came out of the same dressing room. She seemed perfectly natural.

He winked at her. She smiled wanly.

Later that day, after the act had performed, we were having coffee, Hef and me.

He said to me, confidentially, "That Barbie, she's some piece." I nodded.

"Boy," he said, "can she neck."

Neck?

The man who reigned over the Sexual Revolution said, "Can she neck?"

Mercifully, the second season ended. Hefner got bored and went away. Sontag took a job as a thinker at some institute in Aspen. And I was unemployed again.

Only this time, I was thankful.

Joan City

I was out of work. Again. Still. And my depression was beginning to overcome me like an immense smog.

"Let's look at some paintings. It'll make you feel better." Roy Gerber and I were at a museum and he was trying to cheer me up.

"I have to go to the john. I'll see you inside," I said.

In the men's room, at the next urinal, a man said to me, "Aren't you Lester Colodny?"

"Yes. Do you mind? I have serious work to do."

"My name is Rosenberg."

He held his hand out.

I turned away. "First we'll wash. Then we'll shake."

"We read the script you wrote a while ago," said Mr. Rosenberg. "The one with the girl who loses her virginity three times. It was hysterical."

"You read my script?"

"Yes. It was very, very funny."

"Jerry Lewis rewrote it," I said. "Completely. It's unrecognizable from the original."

"I know. Pity. We read it just before he did."

"We? Who's we? And where did you get it?"

"I represent Joan Rivers, the comedienne. A reader at the studio showed it to us when we were over there. We both loved it."

"I'm glad somebody liked it. Give me that reader's address. I'll send her flowers."

"Oh, everybody at Fox liked it."

"So why did they let Jerry Lewis rewrite it?"

"Because that's how they got Jerry to come over."

"But he rewrote the whole thing. The movie is crap. Have you seen it? My only movie credit and it was a complete bomb."

"So what else is new? Listen. How would you like to meet Joan and talk about a play idea she has?"

"Why?"

"Because you're very funny and she's very funny. And the two of you might make a great writing team."

"I've never written a play."

"Neither has she. It might be something worth talking about. We're staying at the Chateau Marmont, before we go on tour."

"Okay, maybe I'll call you. Nice peeing with you."

"That's funny."

"What's funny?"

"'Nice peeing with you.' Wait till I tell Joan."

I walked out of the men's room and found Roy, who was looking intensely at a painting.

"You remember Joan Rivers?" I asked.

"Do I remember her? What a toilet on her. As my mother would say, I wouldn't want to fall into her mouth."

"I just met her manager in the crapper."

"Really? So he hangs out in men's rooms. That's probably where he found that wonderful act to manage."

"He wants me to meet her. He says I should write a play with her."

"Hey, maybe you can catch your balls in your zipper. It would feel a lot better."

"She's that bad?"

"You see that?" he asked. I looked. It was a painting of Saint Sebastian with about a dozen arrows piercing his body.

"What has that got to do with Joan Rivers?"

"You know who did it?"

"Leonardo Da Vinci?"

"No," said Roy. "Joan Rivers."

I met Joan, we talked, we laughed and we agreed to write the play together. And we embarked on a journey that was to have unforeseen consequences. She was working clubs and hotels all over the country and I was traveling with her. We went to work in a fury of invention, outlining the play in two weeks. It was hilarious. We were sure to have an enormous hit on our hands.

For the first time in months, I was able to concentrate on writing. The money I had received from Warner Brothers, for the Jerry Lewis movie and the TV special with Jack Benny, had run out some time earlier. So I begged, borrowed and conned Leonard and Roy into bankrolling me while Joan and I outlined the plot.

It was hilarious; all we had to do was come up with the requisite lines of dialogue. And they were coming like a freight train.

After her second or third show, Joan and I would write. And rewrite. We worked all night, every night, everywhere she could do her stand up comedy. She was funny in a sharp sort of way, coarse, abrasive, but always on the mark. And her fame grew as she toured. Especially when she appeared as an occasional guest on television.

We had a draft in three months. And it was enough to entice Alexander Cohen, a Broadway producer, to Joan's suite. We wandered around, Joan in her gold lamé dressing gown, Rosenberg in his dinner jacket, waiting for this big moment, and me, sipping from a very tall drink in my hand, as Alexander Cohen read the script.

I whispered very softly to Joan, "He hasn't laughed once."

She said quietly, "They say he never laughs. Not even at Neil Simon or Woody Allen."

"Some explanation," I said.

Finally Alexander Cohen finished. He turned the last page of the script and said, "I love it."

"You do?"

"I love it, I love it, I love it. And I'm going to produce it. I'll send you a contract in the morning."

How do you like that? I thought to myself. Three months, working with the wandering Jewess, had finally paid off.

Six weeks later, Alexander Cohen read the pages of the second draft. He was even more enthusiastic. And then he said, "You know, Joan, I think this might be just right for you."

Joan was overcome. I nearly had an aneurism.

"You mean it?" she screeched

"It's you. This play is you," he said.

"You have just made my psychotherapist the happiest woman in the world," she screamed.

"What do you think, Lester?"

I excused myself, went into the bathroom and threw up. All these months, writing a play, and Joan was going to star in it?

I sat there, on the commode, smoking a cigarette. I knew that nothing in the world would keep Joan from doing the part. She was an opening act in Las Vegas about to become a headliner. In her eyes, and her manager's, this was a chance to become a star.

A real starry star.

While Joan and I were making last minute changes in the script, Alexander Cohen was setting up auditions for the show.

The people who read for the play were remarkable. Remarkable in that every single one of them could have, should have, been a star in his or her own show.

Rose Marie (who later played one of the writers on *The Dick Van Dyke Show*) was cast as Joan's mother; Gabe Dell, who had been the leading boy of the Dead End Kids, was chosen to play Joan's husband; and the great comedy actor, Paul Ford, whose list of hits in pictures and plays was astronomical, was to play the oldest living mailman.

Joan was hilariously bringing down stars and politicians on just about every comedy talk show on television. The play had all the earmarks of a smash hit.

Things looked good.

The scenery was designed by the great Ralph Alswang, the lighting by Broadway's eminent Jules Fisher and for costumes, Alexander

Cohen had managed to persuade Ann Roth, whose credits included Jane Fonda's clothes in the hit picture *Klute*, to create the costumes. We were scheduled to open at the Morosco Theatre at Forty-Fifth Street just off Broadway. My fears about Joan as a leading lady were assuaged and we were all excited, overjoyed, practically giddy with excitement when the show went out of town for its first tryout.

I joined the cast and crew for our first date at the National Theater in our nation's birthplace.

The birthplace was the first evidence of an abortion. The critics blew us away. They hated the show. They said it was awful. They said that they couldn't understand how a play with such an outstanding comedy cast, that was so full of jokes, could be so dreary in plot.

But for the folks who loved Joan's stand up material, it was heaven.

For the critics in New York, we were facing certain death.

Just before the week we were scheduled to open in New York, with my hat in my hand and my heart in my shoes, I said to the producer, "I have to talk to you for a few minutes."

"What's on your mind?"

"Mr. Cohen, don't open the show in New York."

"What?"

"Mr. Cohen, please listen to me. If we play this show on the road for fifty-two weeks a year we'll all get rich. Rich beyond our wildest dreams. But if you open it in New York it will close in a heartbeat."

Now, the very fact that a writer would beg not to have his creation opened on Broadway has to tell you something. Hah.

"I don't get you," he said.

"Mr. Cohen, don't you see? Joan is practically doing a stand up routine. Can't you hear it? If you play it on the road, her fans will buy out the show. They'll laugh. They'll scream. They'll tear up the theatres. But if you open it in New York, the critics, who are waiting for Neil Simon's *Prisoner of Second Avenue*, will close us down so fast we'll all catch pneumonia from the draught. I mean it with all my heart, Mr. Cohen. Please, I beg you. Do not open this show in New York. Stay away from New York like the plague."

But just then, Joan came out and said to us both, "Listen to this line. 'If my mother said that to me she'd end up like Mahatma Gandhi. With two black eyes.'"

Mr. Cohen roared. I didn't understand the joke.

It was no use. We were about to plunge into the dragons' mouths.

I stood outside the Morosco theatre on opening night, pacing up and down. I couldn't bring myself to walk in. Every so often I would lean against a door hoping to hear laughter. It was excruciating.

Then the doors opened and people began to pour out of the theater. I leaned over to tie my shoe so I could listen to the comments.

"It is absolutely awful," one woman said emphatically. "It made no sense at all."

A man said to his wife, "Everybody is just standing around on the stage feeding straight lines to Joan Rivers. It's ridiculous." I leaned over to listen to a group of four. A man said, "Let's get a cab and get out of here."

And this was after the first act.

We opened on a Tuesday. We closed on Wednesday.

On Thursday, they tore down the Morosco Theater for an open-air parking lot.

A Walk in the Park

"Where are you going?" asked my daughter Kim, who was living with me.

"For a walk in the park."

"You have got to be kidding. This is New York, Dad. Manhattan. Nobody goes for a walk in Central Park."

"It'll clear my head. I need something to clear my head."

"You go for a walk in the park and you'll get more than your head cleared. If you want to walk take the elevator up to the roof and walk around up there."

"Come on. It can't be that bad."

"No? Go next door and ask our neighbor, Mr. Klein, about the nineteen stitches in his neck he got last week when he went down to get a newspaper."

"Are you trying to tell me—?"

"Not trying, telling. You walk in the park and you'll come home, maybe, on a stretcher. If you're lucky. This is the city. New York Shitty."

"What about the police? Don't they give a person protection?"

"The police are tied up. They're busy with picket duty in front of embassies. Running after hookers. Arresting bums who wash windshields. They have no time for protecting ordinary citizens."

"Come on...I've walked through Central Park a hundred times."

"That was twenty years ago. Before drugs and dealers."

"I'm shocked."

"Shocked? Shocked? You want to know shocked? Go take a walk. In the park. You'll have your brains shocked right out of your skull. Odds are some junkie will hit you with a brick. And that's only if you're lucky because he had to hock his gun to buy heroin. Please don't be upset. You are one of those dear, sweet people who live in the past. It's all over. Finished. Kaput. The world, civilization—it's through. You're looking at Armageddon."

"I can't believe what you're telling me. Armageddon?"

"You know, you should have lived in another time. When there were knights of armor. You would have been Robin Hood with little green shoes that curled up at the toes."

"I'm taking a walk. In the park."

"All right. If you insist, then take a knife from the kitchen. A large one, just in case."

"That's ridiculous."

"Then take an umbrella."

"What are you talking about? It's beautiful out there. And the forecast is for clear skies. Why should I take an umbrella?"

"Not for rain, dumbo. For hitting."

I walked into Central Park at Seventy-Ninth street. It was dusk, and the sun filtering through the trees made the entire setting a peaceful haven and heaven for me as I strolled.

After a bit, I sat down on a bench and contemplated two squirrels squabbling over a piece of discarded bread. It was a scene out of Disney.

A man sat down next to me. He was dressed impeccably, in a stunning vicuna overcoat, kid gloves and shoes shined to a fare-thee-well.

He said to me, "Good evening."

I replied, with a smile, "Good evening."

He leaned over and said softly, "I don't mean to d-d-disturb you, but I w-w-would appreciate it if you w-w-were to h-h-hand me your w-w-wallet and any v-v-v-valuables you m-m-might be c-c-carrying."

I looked up at him in surprise. I said, "I beg your pardon—"

It was then that I noticed he was pointing a small revolver at me.

He whispered, "I s-s-said, your b-b-belongings, your w-w-wallet, and anything of any v-v-value you have at the m-m-moment."

I said, "You want me to—?"

"E-e-exactly."

The incongruity of the scene struck me as ludicrous. It was outrageous. Here I was, broke, an out-of-work writer, eighty thousand dollars in arrears, with seven dollars and thirty-one cents in my pocket, and this very elegantly dressed gentleman (with a stutter) was holding me up.

I said to him, "You realize that this is somewhat—"

He interrupted me. "S-s-sir," he said, "a w-w-week ago I was the owner of a small b-b-business that m-m-manufactured l-l-little g-g-gizmos th-th-that one b-b-blew into and w-when one b-b-blew into th-th-them th-th-they r-r-rolled down and went 'wh-wh-whee.'"

I started to interject but he held up the gun.

"Th-th-then, at a p-p-party, I was introduced to a g-g-gentleman who ench-ch-chanted me. He was a m-man of ind-d-dubitable and unb-b-believable p-p-personality. He c-c-convinced m-m-me that he had a p-p-perfectly v-v-viable enterp-p-prise that would t-t-triple my m-m-money in a f-f-lash.

"I know it was a f-f-foolish th-th-thing to do but I s-s-sold my c-c-company and inv-v-vested the p-p-proceeds in a p-p-play on B-b-broadway. A p-p-play that was an ab-ab-absolutely sure th-th-thing to m-make the r-rest of my l-l-life on earth a p-p-pleasure."

I stared at the man with horror. "The name of the gentleman was?"

"Cohen."

"And the name of the play was *Fun City* with Joan Rivers?"

"How," he stammered, "h-h-how d-d-did you know?"

I held my hand up and reached into my pocket and withdrew the seven dollars and thirty-one cents.

I said, "Good luck with your next victim," and walked away.

N-n-needless to s-s-say, I n-n-never had to use the umb-b-brella.

The Universal Dream

I read through the trade magazines, the want ads, the notices posted on the Writers' Guild bulletin board, every morning for weeks. I had just about run out of unemployment when I heard through the grapevine that there was an opening for a rewrite man or woman at Universal Studios television. The job would pay squat. If I got it. But it least it was something I could go for.

So there I was the next morning, sitting in a waiting room at Universal, along with about fifty or so other burnouts, has-beens and never-would-be's.

When it was my turn to go in, I was introduced to a Mr. Melman.

Mr. Melman was short, squat and bald. He was also hard of hearing. "What have you done?" he bellowed.

"What have I done?" I said.

"What experience do you have?" he shouted.

I couldn't help thinking, if I had any real experience would I be sucking around for a lousy rewrite job? "You want to know if I have any experience?"

"What?"

"You mean what have I done?"

"That's what I asked you."

I said, in a very loud voice, "*The Today Show*. I was a writer on—"

All of a sudden the atmosphere in the room changed from fetid and morose to, well, less fetid.

Mr. Melman sat up in his chair. "*The Today Show*? With Dave

Garroway?"

"Yes."

"Were you a writer on the show where Dave wanted to find out how funny a barrel of monkeys would be?"

I nodded. At least here was a person who had seen the show.

"That was a scream. So, how fast can you write?"

How fast can I write? Again? Was the ghost of Morty Mintz haunting me? If there was a secretary under the desk, I was getting out of there, job or no job.

"Pretty fast," I said.

"Alright. We have a script that has been worked over so many times it looks like it went ten rounds with Muhammad Ali. See what you can do with it and then take it to Mr. Gottlieb by Thursday."

"Today's Thursday."

"What?"

I repeated, louder, "Today's Thursday."

He looked at his calendar. "So it is. All right, Friday."

"You want me rewrite a script in one day? How about Monday? I haven't even read it yet."

"Okay, Tuesday," he agreed.

"Who did you say I should take it to?"

"What?"

"I asked you, who should I take it to when I'm finished?"

"Oh for Christ's sake. You don't know who Gottlieb is?"

"I'm sorry," I said. "Who is he?"

"The head of television here at Universal."

"Oh."

"You'll be paid five thousand. "

Five thousand! Jesus holy moly. Five big ones. Let me at it.

"Yes," I said.

"I have the rewrite for you." It was Tuesday, and I was meeting with Sidney Gottlieb, the head of television for Universal Studios.

"Which rewrite?"

"The one you had Mr. Melman have rewritten for you."

"I don't remember asking Melman to have anything rewritten."

I handed him the one hundred and nine pages I had completed.

He looked at the title page.

"Again? Goddammit. I never liked this idea. I hate it. It won't work. Why does anyone insist on having it rewritten?"

He leafed through the script as if it were a sheaf of corn and said, "Do you think it would work?"

"To tell you the truth—" I began.

He picked up the script and hefted it. "About an hour and a half," he said. "It runs ninety-three minutes."

He could tell it was ninety-three minutes long by holding it?

"You know, I get a lot of admiration. You want to know why? Because I can tell from the weight of a script how long it is, how much it will cost, and who to star in it."

He could tell all that by weighing a script? In his hand? How?

"Does it have a chase?" he asked.

"Don't you remember? It's about two blind people."

"Gotta have a chase. Every picture absolutely must have a chase. Cars, planes, motorcycles, trains, doesn't matter as long as there's a chase. And broken glass. Lots of broken glass. Audiences love broken glass."

"I suppose I could rewrite it so that—"

"What about sex?"

"Sex?"

"You have to have sex. Not too hot. No moofky foofky. But sexy."

"Well, blind people do have sex, so—?"

"That's what sells pizzas and Cokes, my friend. Keeps people on their sofas. A chase, broken glass and sex. Alright, how much?"

"How much?"

"—do you need?"

How much do I need? What was he talking about?

"If you're looking for more than three quarters, I have to tell you, it's too much."

Three? Three quarters? He must think I'm someone else.

"Three quarters of a million?" I asked tentatively.

"That's my top dollar. If you can bring it in for that I'll call Joan and Bob to find out if they're available."

Joan and Bob? Who could he mean? And were they going to play the blind people having sex?

"If either one of them agree to do it, you have a go ahead."

That means a "go."

If I could make this piece of crap for less than three quarters of a million dollars, and if the names he mentioned were—this was unbelievable.

He was on the verge of giving me, a rewrite man, the opportunity of producing and writing a television movie.

I had two options. I could tell him that I was only the rewrite man on the script or I could make out like I was the producer and writer that he thought I was. I decided on the latter.

I said, "I tell you, Mr. Gottlieb, with your abilities you could sell Oreo cookies to cannibals."

"Oreos to cannibals, that's rich. That is rich. I gotta tell the boys at the club. Oreos to cannibals. I like that."

He liked that?

He picked up his phone.

"Get me Joan, then Bob. Then get me—"

He stopped and stared at me for several seconds.

Then he hung the phone up.

"How would you like to work with me?" he said.

I looked around to see if there was anyone else in the room. I knew there wasn't but I looked. There was no one there.

He continued, "Become my right hand man. My brain trust. The hell with making a cockamamie TV picture now and then."

I couldn't believe what I was hearing. He was offering me a job? As his right hand man? I was on the bottom of the ladder in Hollywood. And here he was inviting me to become. . .this was too much.

"I don't know, sir. I had my heart set on—"

"Call me Sidney," he said.

Sidney? Call him Sidney?

I held out my hand. My first mistake. Mr. Gottlieb flinched.

"Never shake hands," he said. "Germs."

"I beg your pardon," I said.

"Never shake hands. That's the way you catch all kinds of diseases."

Diseases. Check. Right. Make a mental note. Never shake hands.

"By the way, who wrote that piece of shit?"

He was referring to the script that I had just handed him (that he had not read) and that he was thinking of getting Joan and Bob to star in and putting up three quarters of a million to produce. What was I going to say?

"Which piece of shit?" I said.

"The thing you just gave me?"

"Oh that." That was it. Shit. I thought very, very, quickly. "Some second-rate creep. We let him go," I answered and held my breath.

"Good thinking. Now, you're a very valuable piece of manpower. Where do I place you in the hierarchy of this company?"

I was being placed in the hierarchy. I felt like pinching myself.

"Have you had much experience in television?"

I crossed my fingers. "I wrote for *The Today Show*."

"*The Today Show*. That's great. I loved that show. Garroway. What a mind."

He loved Garroway. Ychh.

"Just the other day, I let my executive producer go. So, I have an opening. How would you like to exec our television pilots?"

"Exec?"

"Be the boss."

I crossed my toes and said, "I'd love it."

"Done and done," he said emphatically.

Just like that. I was metamorphosed from unemployed to executive. Who in his right mind would believe it?

He reached for his phone. "Emily, come in here."

The door opened and his secretary walked in.

"Emily, I want you to meet the new executive producer of our pilots. . .what was your name?"

I found my new office, on the back lot of Universal, and introduced myself to my new secretary. She was a tall English girl, about twenty-three, with a wonderful smile and the most amazing legs.

"My name is Colodny. Lester Colodny."

"I'm Angela Carruthers," she said.

"You're very pretty," I said. "Can you type?"

She said, "Very slowly."

"Do you take dictation?"

"If you don't speak too quickly."

"Can you make coffee?"

"I make the most heavenly coffee in the world," she said.

"One out of three is a winner. Now, make a pot of coffee and get me the pilot scripts of the shows we have in pre-production."

"I can do that," she said.

The first script was dreadful. Simply dreadful. The second was awful. Worse than the first. Thus far, my newfound excitement about the job was slowly ebbing away.

I sipped my coffee and read the third with growing horror. It was even more appalling than the first two. If the first two scripts hadn't curdled my blood, this one did the job.

In this last script, the lead actress was beaten, mugged and raped. Recovering from the rape she discovered that she had a rare disease. All this was in the first act that took thirteen minutes.

In the second half, her disease was cured but she faced deportation from an unnamed government agency run by her ex-husband who was killed in an explosion caused by—shit. It was terrible.

All this in the pilot script. What was the writer thinking? What could possibly befall this actress in the second episode?

I sat stunned. How could a major studio turn out such rubbish? Such unbelievable shit?

Miss Carruthers came in and announced, "There's a gentleman to see you."

A tall, lanky man in a western outfit with boots, entered. "Gene Coon," he said. He held out his hand.

I said, "Lester Colodny. Can I help you?"

"You're the new man in charge of pilots?"

"I am."

"Well," he drawled, "I'm the guy who will have to rewrite those three ghastly pieces of garbage." He pointed to the scripts on my desk.

"That's not exactly a recommendation," I said.

"They're not exactly works of art," Coon drawled.

"Who wrote the originals?" I asked.

"I'm not certain but there is a rumor around town that Universal has a room with several retarded chimpanzees in it."

"I don't know you but I have the feeling that I can trust you," I said.

"It may be true."

"They stink," I said.

"That's an observation that has some credibility."

"They're terrible."

"Even more credibility."

"I can't believe anyone would even look at them, let alone think about making them."

Coon laughed.

"Have you seen the other shows on the networks?" he said. "Compared to them ours look like they were written by Dickens and produced by Hitchcock."

"I don't watch much television," I admitted.

"Figures. That's why they picked you to do this job."

"Why do you?" I asked.

"Why do I do what?"

"Why do you rewrite these, these, things?"

"Why? Because the studio pays me a shit pot full of money, that's why."

I knew then that I not only liked Coon. At that moment I knew I had a friend.

"Who're the producers and writers of these three abortions?" I asked.

"Well, the Wormsers, Mrs. And Mr., are doing the first, the second has a bunch of loons. And they're still looking for a producer for the third one."

"I just read them," I said. "At least, I read the first few pages. I suppose you have already."

"I never look at horror shows. They make me cringe."

"So how will you rewrite the scripts?"

"You want to know the secret?"

"Yes."

"I'll sit down at my machine, take two pink pills, and type. Meet me in the commissary at twelve, we'll eat."

"What makes you think I'll last that long?"

"Your secretary, Miss Carruthers. What legs," he said and left.

I got up and went to the door. "Come in," I said.

Miss Carruthers entered with a notebook and a pencil. She crossed her legs. They were great legs.

I said, "How long have you worked here?"

"Eleven years," she said.

"Eleven years," I repeated. "Have you ever worked on a picture or a television series that was any good?"

"No."

"Angela, I think I have a problem."

"Please, Mr. Colodny. I'm just a secretary. If you want a psychoanalyst, I have a long list in my directory."

That night, I called Danny Simon, the comedy writer par excellence and crazed ex-roommate.

"Danny," I said, "remember that funny situation comedy you had in mind?"

"Yeah, the family idea of the father and the daughter and the boyfriend who—"

"Yes. I'm heading up the new pilot program at Universal and the stuff I've got—"

"Stinks?"

"I wish they just stank."

"How much?" he asked.

"I'll call your agent. Start writing."

The Cary Grant Story

Every day at about noon, Gene Coon and I broke for lunch and wandered over to the Universal commissary for lunch. We had our own booth with a group of writers and we would exchange gossip and tell jokes that had everybody roaring with laughter. One day, Gene told a joke and we laughed uproariously.

There was a tall man sitting in the booth next to us and when he turned around to tell us what a great joke it was, we realized that sitting next to us was none other than Cary Grant.

He was laughing hysterically.

He said, "That was the funniest joke I've heard in ages. Do you mind if I join you?"

Cary Grant was joining us. We were dumbstruck.

But he was a regular fellow. He joined in with us as if he had been a member of our regular lunch crowd for ages. We accepted him as if he were a writer or a director or anybody other than the biggest movie star on the planet.

One day, Gene suggested that we all join a party he was throwing for his neighborhood that Saturday.

Cary said, "Can I come too?"

We looked at one another.

He said again, "I'd love to come. I have nothing to do on Saturday. I'll bring some wine."

Gene said, "Sure, Cary. Come. About six thirty."

That afternoon, he asked me, "Do you think he meant it?"

"Meant what?"

"About coming to the party?"

"I don't know," I said. "Sounded like it."

That night Gene told his wife, "You'll never believe who might be coming to our party Saturday night."

"Who?" she said.

"Cary Grant."

There was at least ten seconds of silence. Then a scream. "Cary Grant is coming to my party?" she shouted.

"Our party," Gene said.

But she was out the door and announcing to all the neighbors that Cary Grant was coming Saturday night. Immediately, eight wives made appointments at their beauty parlors for Saturday afternoon.

Saturday was a mad scramble. Everyone got dolled up for Cary Grant. The wives wore their best dresses and pant suits, the men got out to their best slacks and sports shirts. A brand new grill, costing several hundred dollars, was installed in Gene's back yard and everybody waited for the arrival of—Mr. Cary Grant.

He arrived in a convertible wearing old clothes—a pair of slacks, a tee shirt—and carrying a case of wine. "Hello everybody," he said.

We all stood around, open mouthed. He was gorgeous. Wonderful. Magnificent. He was—Cary Grant.

He carried in his case of wine, opened it and put half the bottles in the fridge. Then he said, "I'm starved."

The mad dash for the grill started two seconds later. Everyone wanted to make him a steak.

He said, "Make my burger medium well."

Twenty minutes later he had the whole crowd gathered around him and he was telling the same jokes we told at lunch, plus a few new ones. We laughed (even though our wives knew the punch lines). We played games. Before you knew it, he was one of the bunch.

The women ran home and changed into normal clothes. The men put away their dress-up duds. It was one, grand old-fashioned bust out of a party. Three hours later, Cary was at Gene's sink, wiping and drying dishes, and joined in singing with the half-drunk crowd that was perched around the kitchen. It was midnight.

We sat around in the backyard while he told us stories of how he had started, how he was cast as an extra and then as a heavy and then how he got his first starring role. We were entranced.

Then he said, as he glanced at his watch, "Got to go. Playing tennis with Hitch tomorrow morning. But I want you to all know, this has been the most fun I've had since I started in Hollywood."

The next day, Gene told me, he and his wife were shopping in the local deli when a woman approached her.

"Hey," she said. "How was your party last night?"

"Not bad."

"Who was there?"

"Oh, Lester and a date, Gene and me, Mort and Maralyn, Joan and Marvin, Hildy and Martin, Louise and Fred, Maxine and Max, Sid and Helen, and...oh yes," she added with total nonchalance, "Cary Grant."

Sidney's Secret

I woke up, six months later, exhilarated. Euphoric. All was right with my world. Languidly, I stretched and breathed in the wonderful mountain air. What a marvelous morning. Nothing could go wrong on a day that started like this.

On this crisp, beautiful morning, the birds sang and all was wonderful in the universe. Somehow, with God and Gene Coon's help, we had managed to improve the scripts on the three shows and get the ratings up where they competed with all the other programs.

In spite of Sidney Gottlieb's constant imbecilic meddling, I had accomplished the near impossible. I was soaring. And for once in my life, I felt I deserved it. All of it.

No, sir. I didn't get this kind of a feeling very often.

The phone rang.

Make believe I died. That I went to Africa on a surprise safari.

"Forget it," I said.

It rang again.

"Forget it! Let it ring," I said. "I walk around with butterflies in my belly too much these days."

The phone rang again and again.

I cannot come to the phone this morning. I am very busy breathing. And stretching. And smelling. And living.

The phone stopped ringing. Whoever it was had given up.

I grinned a wide filet of a grin. A grin that started at my mouth and spread around my ears to the back of my neck, then down my spine to my hips and around my stomach and down my legs to my toes. A super grin.

In a few minutes I would brew a pot of coffee. Not that instant crap, but a real, live cup of coffee. Without a cigarette. Today I might even quit smoking.

I would shower. A long, hot, steaming shower. Then I would shave, get dressed, put the top down on my car and drive out to the beach.

Fuck the job. Fuck it all. Today was a day of days. Not a day to be cooped up in an office.

Today was one of those days the gods reserved for people who had temporarily forgotten. People who had been so busy consuming the world that they had forgotten that birds sang and flowers smelled and faces grinned.

The coffee was just beginning to perk as I finished shaving. The odors of freshly brewed coffee beans and shaving lotion swirled together, giving me a heady feeling of who-cares-what-happens-today, I am one with the world.

I went out to pick up the newspapers and the trade papers and it was then that I saw the headline, "UNI TV Head Tells All" on the front page of *Variety*, the bible of the industry.

I sat down on my front step and read the column written by Army Archard, confidante of the rich and fabulous, the writer whose column had caused more trouble and heartache in the business for twenty years.

> Sid Gottlieb, that infamous manipulator turned creator, told me today that the secret of Hollywood was all in the word. "The word is what counts," he said as

he sipped his early morning coffee after two sets of singles tennis at the Beverly Hills Hotel. "The secret of my success is that I am on top of all the TV scripts that come out of my studio. I read them every night before I go to bed" (*He read the scripts? The last thing he read was the outside of a cereal box.*) "and use my trusty green pencil to rewrite everything that is filmed on my lot."

It went on and on about how he created the three series that were now climbing up the charts and showing the other studios how and why TV series can be successful.

That terrible egomaniac. That dreadful lunatic. That prick. He had to mouth off to the biggest *yachnah* in the gossip business, who wrote the column that everybody read. Now we were in the toilet. If we weren't before, we were now in. Solidly. In hard chunks.

Why didn't we just kill him? Why couldn't the people who did the work all just surround him in the commissary and let someone stick a knife in his black heart? The police wouldn't suspect anyone of the in-group because we all ostensibly loved and adored our leader. Didn't he pay us handsome salaries? Didn't we all have big studio cars? Weren't we all rich and famous because of him? Because of his great creative brain? Which of us could possibly have a motive? It would be the perfect crime.

The only way the police could solve the crime would be to identify someone's lip-prints on the corpse's ass.

By the time I arrived at my office it was eleven o'clock and all hell had broken loose. My secretary's outer cubicle looked like a hotel room scene in a Marx Brothers movie.

There were at least a dozen maniacs pressed into that tiny space, all of them shouting at my secretary who was pressed against the window, fending them off with a stapling gun.

"Help," she screamed, as she saw my face in the doorway. "They're going to smother me to death."

A horde of panic-stricken producers, writers, agents and technicians turned as if a master puppeteer had pulled all their strings at once. They stared slack-jawed at me for a long silent beat. It was weird. In that one magic instant, I slipped past their idiotic stares and locked the door of my office.

Buzzing Miss Carruthers on the intercom, I told her to bring a gallon of black coffee and a carton of cigarettes, and to start sending the besiegers in one by one; no one to get more than five minutes.

I had instructed Miss Carruthers to send them in one at a time, but two of them slithered in at the first opening of the door. A writer, Milton Pyne, and a producer, Stanley Z. Coen. They both began to holler and tear their hair at the same time. I couldn't understand either one.

"Hold it. Hold it," I shouted. "What's wrong, Milton?"

"I was here first," Stanley whined.

I made a mental note to have one of those take-a-number machines installed in my secretary's office.

"All right," I said resignedly, "Stanley is first."

Stanley Z .Coen, a tall, mustachioed television producer, began to pace the floor, biting his well manicured cuticles as he whimpered out his sad tale. "That fucking little shithead director, Jeremy Weiss, is three days behind schedule. Three days. Three whole days. Gottlieb will have my ass in a sling, Lester. What should I do?"

"Why did you wait until now to tell me? You must have known he was falling behind before today, didn't you?" I said.

"He kept telling me he was doing the difficult scenes first," Stanley moaned.

"Oh, come off it," I said. "You should have fired his ass after the first day's work."

"But he's a very fine director. I can't just fire a director like Jeremy Weiss."

I couldn't decide whether to punch the sniveling creep in the mouth or throw him out of the office. Instead, I took a long drag on my cigarette and answered softly, "Stanley, you must not try to bullshit me. I am the king. One does not bullshit the king. I happen to know that Jeremy Weiss and you have the same agent. That's why you can't fire him. Now, as of this moment, he is canned."

Stanley's face turned a strange color of green as I buzzed my secretary. "Get Mort Zarcoff to take over on Stage One and have Weiss paid off," I commanded, "and get your ass in here with my coffee."

(When I had interviewed her, back when I started this job, I had said, Can you make coffee?"

"I make the most heavenly coffee in the world," she had said. Now, I needed that coffee.)

Stanley Z. Coen fucked up by hiring Jeremy Weiss because Jeremy played tennis with Stanley's agent, Aldon Shwimmer. Jeremy fucked up, but because he played tennis with Aldon, and because Aldon beat

Jeremy daily and collected untold sums from him, Stanley Z. Coen was afraid to fire Jeremy. Now the whole affair turned into a pile of crap and I ended up walking behind the elephant with a shovel.

No one was going to ask why I pulled Jeremy Weiss off the picture. They were only going to know that I had him thrown off the set.

Within twenty-four hours, I was going to be persona non grata with the Directors Guild, not to mention every asshole writer, actor and producer who played tennis at the goddamn Beverly Hills Club.

Colodny, the heavy.

Colodny, the killer.

Colodny, the hired assassin.

A couple more Stanley Z. Coen-type goodies and I would be as popular as a hit-man for the Mafia. This was the first one of the day and already I was feeling nauseous.

"Stanley," I said, with gritted teeth, "I don't ever want to see Jeremy Weiss or your fucking agent on this lot again. You hear?"

"But, I—"

"Or I'll shove his tennis racquet right up his ass."

I had already turned to the other man in the room. Milton Pyne was always very tired from writing seven nights a week for the past ten years. "Yes, Milton?" I prompted softly as Stanley Z. Coen slunk out of the room. (I made a mental note to ask him, sometime in the near future, why he dropped the "h" out of Coen).

Milton was a writer who looked at least two hundred years old. He had already written himself out twice in the service of the Universal

Studios Television department and I expected him to drop dead right there in the middle of the room.

He looked at me through two slits and opened his mouth but no sound came out.

"What is it, Milton?" I said, a little louder, hoping to rouse him from his daze.

"Did you see that interview in the *Times*?" Milton whispered.

Oh balls, not you, too.

"Yes, I saw it," I answered in what I hoped was a nonchalant tone of voice.

"So did my wife, Lester. She wants me to resign from the job."

"Your wife? What has the interview got to do with your wife?"

"Lester, don't yell, please. I don't feel too good."

The door opened and my secretary slithered in with a carafe of coffee and a carton of cigarettes.

"It's a lunatic asylum out there. It's so crowded they're breaking the furniture," she wailed.

"Okay. Get Coon in here right away. You want some coffee, Milton?"

Milton shook his head sorrowfully as he watched my secretary's ass squeeze out the door.

I tore the carton open, broke a fresh pack and sipped the hot, black, wonderful liquid.

"Now, what is this about your wife?" I asked, as if I didn't already know. Milton Pyne had been so busy typing scripts he hadn't so much as squeezed his wife's tits for three months.

"Ethel is furious. She says that you use people like me. She says you make chopped liver out of people. She wants me to quit and take her on a cruise."

This was real trouble. The situation comedy series of television is the most unique form of theatrical endeavor. It is the wild animal cage of the circus, and the head writer is the lion-tamer.

A head writer must be a combination of a genius, computer, and megalomaniac. He has to have the constitution of a hippopotamus and the libido of a monk. He has to continually find new ways to write the same stupid, outrageous inanities week after week, for months at a time, and convince himself that he is creating something exciting and fresh and different in every episode. Above all, he has to convince himself that what he is doing is art when he knows it is tripe.

I would really be up the creek if Milton Pyne went to the bathroom, not to mention on a cruise.

"As soon as the season is over," I said, "I promise you and your wife a three months' vacation in Europe. All expenses paid, Milton. I swear it." I didn't know where I would get the money for it but what the hell. I was desperate.

"She says if I don't quit, today, she's going to divorce me," Milton said and turned toward the window.

That goddamned stupid son-of-a-bitch Gottlieb. All he had to do was mention a few names in that frigging interview. All he had to say was—it was no use. The shit had already hit the fan.

"Milton," I whispered, as I got up from out from behind my desk and walked over to the forlorn little man. I put my arms around his shoulders and squeezed him. "I need you. Like I need blood, right now. If you leave me, I will drive out to Forest Lawn Cemetery and lie down in the grass for a fitting."

He turned and smiled at me. It was weak but a smile. "All right. But only for you, Lester . Only for you," he said, and slouched toward the door.

"Thank you, Milton. And I'll call Ethel and tell her about Europe."

"That won't be necessary, Lester," he almost cried. "I think we're washed up anyhow."

Milton and Ethel Pyne? They had been married for more than twenty years. It was one of the seven wonders of Hollywood. A good marriage in Loonytuneville.

"I found cigar butts in the car ashtray."

"So? What has that got to do with—?"

"She screws young actors, Lester. She goes around the Strip during the day and picks up guys. In Schwab's, at the market, anyplace. Every place." He started to cry.

"How do you know this is true?"

He looked up at me with the saddest, reddest eyes I had ever seen. "I followed her. She's even fucking unemployed extras, Lester." He began to cry harder.

"So what's this about a cruise?"

"I guess she's feeling guilty and had to have a copout. Forget it. I have to go back to the machine." He slumped out of the office and I lit a cigarette, cursing my studio head, as Gene Coon came slouching in.

"What's up, suck-ass?" Coon grinned. "Your outer office looks like the toilet overflowed."

"All right, enough," I growled. But inwardly I smiled. I just adored this skinny bastard from Shirley, Iowa. He was my ace in the hole. My saver. My life's breath. Whenever things really went bad, I called for Gene Coon, the world's fastest everything. He was a super fixer-upper. Name it, Gene Coon could do it.

But he was temperamental and touchy. So I saved him for the tough ones. And this was a really tough one and I knew that Coon knew it.

"Milton quit?" Coon smirked as he opened my liquor cabinet and poured himself a water glass full of brandy.

"Not yet, but God knows about all those other nuts out there."

"Send 'em in," Gene laughed, as he added two spoonfuls of coffee to the brandy. He sprawled full length on my couch and began to sip the drink, chuckling to himself. "I have the *Times* delivered every morning, too," he said.

I pressed the intercom buzzer twice and the door opened, admitting Phyllis and Morty Wormser, a man and wife producer-writer team. Phyllis was the man. (At least she played the part of a man.)

"We came to say good-bye, Mr. Colodny," she said as her husband stole a pack of cigarettes off my desk.

But she had called me "Mr." and I knew I had an edge in this confrontation. I rose and held out my hand. "Goodbye, Phyllis."

"You really don't want to know why or what for?" she asked incredulously.

"My dear Phyllis. We all learned to read when we were little," I replied, making an effort to keep from sounding too sarcastic. "Education is free for everyone in this country. Unfortunately, psychiatry is not. And if you insist on chucking five thou a week because a moron has bruised your ego, then all I can say is '*bon voyage*.'"

"Sid Gottlieb didn't create our show." Her voice was just a little lower than that which dogs could hear. "Morty and I made that show up right out of our own family. From our own kids. How dare he say that he created the—?"

"Phyllis," I interrupted. "Phyllis, at the end of every episode, what does it say in great big letters?"

"Created, Produced and Written by Phyllis and Morty Wormser," Coon drawled from the couch. "Big as a dinosaur's ass."

"But who'll believe it at Chasen's after that article?" she demanded of Coon.

"Chasen's?" I shouted. "Fifty million people see that fucking credit every week, twenty-six weeks a year, not including summer reruns. And you're worried about what they'll say at Chasen's? The next time you go to dinner at Chasen's I'll send along a projector and a can of film and you can show it to your friends. You want me to take an ad out in *Variety*?"

I made out like I was furious. The poor bitch and her mouse of a husband. But Morty was already snitching another pack of cigarettes from my carton and furtively leaving the office. There was a long moment of silence broken only by the racket of voices outside the office door.

Phyllis said to Coon, "Did you finish that rewrite I asked you for?"

"Three hours ago, sweetie. It's already typed, duplicated and stapled."

Phyllis turned red, then purple, then ashen. "Let's go, Morty. There's no satisfaction to be gained from these. . .these. . .sycophants."

As the door closed behind them, Gene rolled off the couch, hysterical.

"I thought she'd bust a gasket," he howled.

"Cool it," I hissed as the door opened to admit Danny Simon's agent, Freddie Freid.

"Lester, Lester, Lester," Freddie cooed.

I glanced over at Coon. Coon winked back at me, meaningfully. It was a three-Lester hello. Freddie Freid had arrived with a bagful of problems.

I stood up and held my hand out. "How are you, Freddie?"

"How am I? How should I be?" he mewled, as he held his hand to his cheek. "Oh, Lester, Lester, Lester, what would us agents do without a Lester Colodny?"

"We agents," I couldn't resist correcting him.

"We, us, what would we do? Oh, Lester, Lester, Lester. You're beautiful."

He turned to Coon. "Gene, I ask you. Is that Lester beautiful?"

"Stunning," Coon snorted from the couch. "If he was a girl, I'd hump him."

"Fun-nee. Fun-nee," Freddie Freid roared, then turned to me and leaned across my desk. "So, what's new, Lester?"

Freddie Freid always asked "what's new" when he was about to tell you something terrible.

And I knew what it was all about.

"What am I going to do about Danny?" he wailed.

"What are you going to do about Danny?" I exploded. "You'll do nothing, that's what."

"Lester," he perspired. "He is reading that *yachnah*'s column as we speak. I have a bad kidney, Lester. My sacroiliac is killing me. And I'm not getting anything from my spleen. Lester, Lester, Lester, what am I going to do with Danny?"

Gene Coon excused himself. "I have to go rewrite," he said.

Freddy sat down in Coon's place on the sofa and put his head in his hands.

A Funny Thing Happened

The Odd Brothers

I thought any confidence Danny ever had in himself, as a man, or as a talent, disappeared down the tubes when he received that telephone call from his brother Neil in New York. He was calling to read Danny the reviews of his play.

"Danny, there's a line from the box office all the way around the block. The *Times* says it will run for years. And three major studios have already made offers for the motion picture rights."

"Congratulations, kid, I hope I can get in to see it soon."

"Danny," Neil had said. "Please. Fly in tonight. Bring Irma and the kids. I'll spring for the whole tab. Danny, I'm rich, I made it, Danny."

"I'd love to, kid. But these shit heads at Universal have me writing everything in the studio including the lunch menus."

That was Monday morning. In the afternoon, the stock market plunged fifty points and when Danny called his business manager in a panic, he discovered that the man had been arrested the night before in a Santa Monica gay bar for trying to pick up a vice-squad detective. He frantically put in a direct call to the broker only to learn that he had been arrested for swimming nude on a public beach.

The next morning, Danny, his stomach distended with anxiety, tried to discreetly break wind during a production meeting and crapped in his pants.

Within minutes, his big-mouthed secretary told the story to another girl and the story had spread hysterically all over the lot.

Embarrassed and mortified, he fired the secretary, got into his car and drove off the lot and into the rear end of a police car.

The rookie cop, irate and frightened, booked him on a charge of suspected drunken driving. And when Danny finally got his attorney's office on the phone, he was told that the lawyer was busy in Santa Monica trying to bail out his business manager and broker. So a broken Danny Simon spent the night in the tank at the Van Nuys police station.

My secretary stuck her head in. "Excuse me, but Mr. Simon, your number one pain-in-the-behind is here."

"I better get out," said Freddy Freid. "How can I get out?"

"Go through my bathroom."

In a flash, the agent was gone.

Danny Simon shambled in and sat down on the couch. "I'm finished," he mumbled.

"Thank God," I sighed.

"Done," said Danny.

"You are three weeks late but I know it was worth it. Let me see the pages."

He looked up at me through bloodshot eyes, like a rabbit that had just been bitten by a dog.

"Don't you hear me?" he wailed.

"I hear you. And I love you for sticking it out."

"You never listen," Danny screamed. "I'm done. Finished. Washed up. I'm a has-been. I have no talent. I'm a nothing. No thing. I am shit."

I stared across my desk at this sobbing forty-five year old child/man and wondered whether I should leap across the desk and rip his throat out or just hug him.

"Do you mean to tell me," I croaked, "that we have been paying you five thousand dollars a week, plus your agent's commission, and—how far did you get with the script?"

"Five pages."

"That's a thousand dollars a page?"

There was murder and mayhem in my heart. I was beyond rage. "What happened?" I asked. "Wait a minute, I don't really want to know because I really don't care. I only wish you would contract leprosy so I could tell the legal department and Sidney Gottlieb that your fingers fell off after ten pages. I could smash your face, Danny, and tell Mr. Gottlieb you were so loyal that you tried to type with your nose.

"Why, Danny? Why did you take money from me. . .from the studio. . .and four months later you come in and tell me that you have completed five pages? Why, Danny? Why have I stuck with you, through thick and thin for all these years? Tell me, Danny, why?"

He looked at me blankly.

"I represented you. I sold you to *The Show of Shows*, with your brother, where you fucked up by telling everybody how to write. You told Larry Gelbart how to write. You told Mel Brooks how to write. You told all the writers including Woody Allen how to write. I sold you to all those shows—Red Buttons, Milton Berle, all of them. And when I couldn't sell you, I hired you, every time. And you fucked up. You always fucked up. Why? Why did you fuck up again? I want to know."

"I got a call from New York," Danny said quietly. "From my brother."

"I know your brother," I said. "He was your partner. I represented both of you at the Morris office."

"Well, he wrote a play. *The Odd Couple*. And it's a hit. A great big fucking, smash hit on Broadway. I spend my life writing junk shit for junk shit television situation comedies that aren't even funny and my kid brother has another enormous hit, a huge hit, a fucking play on Broadway."

"I know your brother. He is some writer. I read the reviews."

"He is some writer? He is some writer? My brother, who never finished his homework because he couldn't put a sentence together and I had to write everything for him, he has a colossal hit. The third one in a row. And who do you think wrote the first twelve pages of *The Odd Couple* that he sold to Broadway?"

"So why didn't you finish it?" I shouted.

He didn't answer me. Just looked at me through crusted eyes. "I am a flop," cried Danny. "Flip flop. Flip flap flop. Flippety, flocky, shitty, cocky, flop flee flop. Floppissimo."

"Wait a minute," I said.

"No. You wait. For all these years I have been writing television programs. Shit cocky doody. That's what. All these years and a hundred million jokes later. And what happens. I ask you, what happens?

"My kid brother, an ordinary, plain guy sits down and writes a hysterical play. Not makes a bird cage or a trellis. He writes a play that is a fucking killer hit. With screams from the audience.

"And it's all your fault. Because it is the Lester Colodnys and all the other ass holes in the world who suck me in with long-term contracts and deals with big bonuses. Always coming up to me, buttering me up to do another shitty series and then still another series.

"So how can I, who knows more about comedy writing than any other human being in the history of mankind, including Sid Caesar, Milton Berle and Goodman Ace, ever find the time to write a play when all of you are all the time juicing me, wringing out my brains?"

"Are you finished?" I shouted. "Are you through? I sucked you in? I conned you? I buttered you up? Nobody, did you hear that word, nobody, in this town would hire you to change their typewriter ribbons because all you do is rewrite every fucking word they write. And I, like a schmuck, give you a choice assignment. I make you the head writer on a hit series. At top dollar. At five thousand dollars a week. Not per show. Per week. Out of the goodness of my heart.

"You schmuck, you creep. You fucking piece of shit. Go home. Get out of here."

Danny walked to the window and dove out.

What a bad break. I had no luck. I hired a writer because his agent, his friends, his wife and God knows who all else begged me to give him one more chance.

Not only did I give in, despite my every instinct to ignore them all, not only did I relent, I gave him a contract for five thousand dollars a week.

Not only did he not come through and write a dandy script, he shows up four months later, with a measly five pages, and jumps out of my goddamned window.

He jumps out my office window.

My office is on the ground floor.

A Munster Idea

Why should I have complained? I had a fancy job. I hobnobbed with stars.

But I produced drek.

Just about everybody in the business produced trash but it was taking its toll on me. In spite of the fact that most television was simply garbage and not even creative garbage, I still had a vestige of the old Lester in me.

And I longed for that one show, that one program, that would take me over the top into what the critics called great.

Then Sidney Gottlieb called me in and said, "Hey Lester. Forget about supervising. What do you think about screening a bunch of old movies and coming up with some kind of TV series based on them?"

"Sure," I said enthusiastically. I was very disgusted with Danny Simon and his ilk. This could be interesting. "What movies?"

"*Frankenstein, Frankenstein Meets the Wolfman*, and *Frankenstein and Dracula*."

The smile froze on my face. He didn't notice. He'd already left the room.

I called Coon and told him about it.

"You're putting me on," he said. "When do you start?"

"I started already."

"Then maybe I'd better get you some hemlock for dinner."

After screening the films Universal owned, I threw up. Then I came up with a brainstorm.

What would happen if I were to make a family out of the Frankenstein pictures? I could give him a wife who was straight out of Dracula and an uncle who was a steal from the Wolfman. I could add a creepy kid, but I needed something to balance the weirdo equation so the audience would go along with it.

That was it.

The family of weirdos would have a crazy grandfather and a normal teenage niece. And the whole family would be living in an ordinary house on an ordinary block in an ordinary city. It seemed like a perfect set-up for a hundred story lines.

I wrote until dawn. Then I raced into work.

I waited for Gene in his office. He walked in the door and I crowed, "I think I licked it. Read this."

"Already? Can I have a cup of coffee first?" he asked.

"I'll make the coffee, you read."

Twenty minutes later, he looked up. "I think you should see a doctor."

"A doctor?"

"Either you have lost your mind or this is one of the wackiest ideas I have ever read. These pages are a scream. I don't know what kind of a scream but definitely a holler."

I took my pages to Sid.

"Already?" he said.

"Just read."

He was no pushover so when he started to laugh at the first page, I knew I was on to something.

Finally, he put down the outline I had written and said, "In my life, I have never read anything like this. I think you are either a very creative person or we should have you locked up. What'll you call it?"

"I'm thinking of *At Home With The Ghouls*."

He thought for a little, then said, "No, no, doesn't work."

"How about, *The Ghouls Next Door*?"

He shook his head. We both thought some more.

I said, "Wait, I've got it. How about *The Munsters*?"

"As Henry Higgins said in Pygmalian, 'I think you've got it,'" he said. "Leave these with me. I'll get them to Mr. Wasserman tonight." (Lou Wasserman was the president and CEO of the studio.) "I'll take them to his house in Malibu and wait while he reads them. Either you'll have a deal by tomorrow or both of us will be thrown off the lot."

"You really like it that much?"

"It's tremendous," he said. "I think."

The next morning, the phone rang early. I grabbed it.

It was Sid. "I know you're not going to believe this but the boss said you have a green light to make a pilot film."

I was thrilled.

"He's giving you twenty-five thousand."

I was horrified.

"Twenty-five thousand? How can I make a pilot for that amount of money with a script, a set, and actors. Remember actors? The people who say all those words we make up?"

"I know, I know. Look, I think the show you have is fantastic. It's a panic. But Lew is the boss. He said twenty-five. So take your best shot."

That night, I conned two writers into writing a script on spec. (That means, if we sold it they'd get paid.) Meanwhile I scrambled through actors' books looking for someone, anyone, who could play Frankenstein. I put in a call to Eddie Blum, a casting director and an old friend from the William Morris Agency, in New York.

"What was the name of that actor who played the cop on *Sergeant Bilko?*" I asked.

"Fred Gwynne. Why?"

"I've got a series idea for him."

"Not a chance," Eddie answered. "He told me he will never, ever, go to the coast for even a walk on. He hates California."

But I was undaunted. "Can you give me his telephone number?" I said.

That night I called Fred Gwynne in Sneedens Landing, New York.

"Mr. Gwynne, my name is Lester Colodny. I'm a producer of new television comedy shows here at Universal—"

"Thank you but no," he said.

"Mr. Gwynne, please. Give me a few minutes."

"I don't mean to be rude, Mister Colodny, but I will never again play in a situation comedy. It is too grueling."

"Mr. Gwynne—"

"Where are you planning on shooting this?" he asked.

"Out here. In California."

"Impossible. Not only will I not play in a situation comedy, I won't go to Hollywood, it's too crazy out there."

"Please, let me tell you about the part," I insisted.

"I already told you—"

"Let me just read you the first three pages," I pleaded.

"Read me the first page."

I read him the first page. There was a long pause.

He said, "Read me two more."

I read two more pages.

He said, "Send me the rest of the script and a first class ticket. If the rest of the script is as funny, I'll come out to do a test."

I was thrilled. The writers had scored.

I reported to Sidney J. Feinberg Jr., Universal's Vice President for Finance, that the actor Fred Gwynne had agreed to come to California to perform in a pilot film for *The Munsters* and that he should make a deal that would pay his airfare and compensation for the pilot film and further compensation in the event the pilot were sold.

Then I sent the script, written by Norm Leibman and Ed Hass, to Mr. Gwynne and called in a lot of markers I had with people on the lot. If Fred Gwynne agreed to make the pilot, I would manage to scrounge up a director and a crew. There was no budget for costumes so I waded through wardrobe departments everywhere. I chose an ordinary house in a very ordinary neighborhood on the back lot and waited.

Three days later, my secretary ran in waving a telegram. It was from Gwynne. He agreed to come out and make the pilot.

Now, I had to cast the rest of the family. And after much wrangling and cheating and lying to agents and managers, I cast Joan Marshall as the wife (later replaced by Yvonne DeCarlo), Beverly Owen as the neice and Al Lewis as the uncle.

We had one day to shoot whatever we could, and so Fred stood in front of the camera, in full costume, and spoke directly to the audience. He told them what the show was about, he explained the characters and even some of the plots.

Then we shot the first three scenes. It was all we could afford.

Fred wished me good luck and went back to Sneedens Landing.

A month later, I was driving onto the lot when the aforementioned Boss, the major domo of the studio, Lew Wasserman, was driving off.

He gestured to me to roll down my window.

"We sold your fucking show," he laughed. "I don't understand it but we sold it. Congratulations."

I was so excited, I almost crashed my car. My hands were shaking and I had butterflies in my stomach. I realized I hadn't been this juiced about anything in years.

I called Gene.

"You're kidding me, right?" he said.

"I just got it from the mouth of God himself."

"Congratulations."

"I've been waiting a long time for this," I said.

"Well then, enjoy it while it lasts. This is Hollywood, Lester. You may never get to shoot another piece of film on it."

A week later, Sid Gottlieb called me into his office.

"Lester," he said, "I have something I want to talk to you about. We're giving *The Munsters* to Connelly and Moser to produce."

Joe Connelly and Bob Moser were two producer/writers who had produced and written *Leave It to Beaver* and other shows. But they were schlock.

The Munsters was funny, it was bright, it had a touch of class. Why in the world would they give the show to those two hacks?

I sat there with my mouth open. I couldn't believe what I was hearing.

"The networks want an experienced team," he said, "And Lew Wasserman told me that Connelly and Moser were eminently acceptable."

I rose from my chair and said, "Connelly and Moser? Those two over-the-hill make-believe—"

"You're walking on very thin ice."

I couldn't help it. I completely lost it. "I can't believe you're telling me this," I shouted. "I work my ass off, I create a show from some dreadful movies and make it into a great comedy. I hire two writers who worked for me, on the come, to write a show to prove that it works. I helped write it. I produced it. I cast it. I did everything but put the film in the can. And you have the effrontery to tell me that you are taking the show away from me and giving it to—"

Gottlieb said. "You are management. At Universal, management creates, makes up, sells, but does not take credit."

"But that show came out of me," I screamed. "It's mine. And you're going to take away my creation and give it to a couple of—?"

He said, "You don't understand, do you?"

"No," I thundered. "I do not understand," and I stormed out of his office.

I was blind with rage. I stalked all the way back to my bungalow with tears in my eyes. It was then that I saw two men painting out the sign on my parking spot. It was that fast.

Miss Carruthers was already piling my things into cartons. She couldn't bring herself to look at me.

Minutes later, two studio guards came to my office.

"Sorry, Mr. Colodny," said one.

"What are you sorry about?" I asked.

"We've come to escort you off the lot. Orders from the front office."

I was not only not going to produce *The Munsters*, I was about to become unemployed. Again.

Lester ready to take the world on in NY, once he gets his makeup finished (above).

Lester (right) in Florida with Wally Olesen, then VP of Advertising with Xerox.

Lester (third from the right, facing the camera) on a balcony in Bulgaria.

Lester's roadside encounter with Jerry Lewis that led to *Which Way to the Front?* immortalized in a watercolor.

Lester speaking at a roast of Steve Wynn at the Golden Nugget. Red Buttons is in the middle, taking a sip of his drink.

Frank Sinatra pretending to pay off Steve Wynn for more towels. From a 1981 calendar produced by Wynn's Casinos.
Commercial distribution rights held by Lester Colodny.

Liz, Lester and Bob Hope

Lester directing Frank Sinatra, from an unknown newspaper, circa 1980.

This is believed to be a unique image used to illustrate an event. Used under fair use laws.

FROM LEFT TO RIGHT: Frank Sinatra, John P. Carey, executive producer, and Lester Colodny, director of JPC Visuals, Inc.

Sinatra giving Wynn a play slap across the face.

From a 1981 calendar produced by Wynn's Casinos.
Commercial distribution rights held by Lester Colodny.

Liz and Lester... The early years...

Lester and Liz with three very important dignitaries.

Costume prize-winners Liz and Lester.

NEIL SIMON

Monday Oct. 10th

Dear Lester,

    Sorry I didn't answer you sooner but I just got back from London and Paris last night and just got through reading both your letters this morning.

    I was in Europe about three weeks and saw the "Odd Couple" open in Paris where it was a smash. Of course my French is limited but every time they said "Frere Jacques" I laughed like hell.

    To business. I love you, I adore you, you're one of my dear friends and I would love to keep it that way. I don't want to do the television series. I could go in to the million and one reasons I hate all the shows I see, but they really aren't worth discussing. "The Drumbeater" is a basically funny idea but needs a great deal of rewriting. I am not prepared to do it nor will I allow anyone else to do it. It belongs in that great file in the sky marked "Good Tries".

    I quite honestly feel Danny's show is the kind that is much better suited to a long run TV series. It has warmth, charm and reality. "The Drumbeater" should be a one shot special or even a feaxture film. The Jew has spoken.

    I go into rehearsals on Monday with "The Star Spangled Girl" so any future correspondence concerning "The Drumbeater" will have to be conducted with my nine year old Ellen, or with three year old Nancy, providing you draw out everything with crayon.

                       My best to you,

                                Doc

A Letter from Neil Simon to Lester Colodny
concerning "The Drumbeater"

A 1984 letter to Lester from Estelle Harris (*Seinfeld*)

Estelle Harris today (right)
Picture used with permission of Estelle Harris

Estelle Harris

2/26/84

My Dear Lester,

I've been laughing for three days!

When any of my family pass me in the kitchen, mumbling, "I'm not eating home" or "I need money" or "You're getting too fat," what retort do I throw back at them?

Giggles. Nothing but giggles and smiles of contentment--- because of you Lester.

I know what a great director you are. Remember our Golden Nugget shoot? Working with you was a joy.

You make an actor want to do her best. Yiou glow with creativity. You become a friend---an understanding, sensitive, electric, colorful and wonderful ally. Couldn't be better.

But as a writer, too?

I'm flipping.

I tell your sayings like they're from the bible---like even from Shakespeare.

"My sister called but couldn't talk."

"My wife goes to Bendels instead of Leohmans."

"My postman has to get a truss…"

"It rolls off my tongue like seltzer."

   Lester, if you want, when I see you, I'll quote you verbatim. I'm using whole passages as audition monologues. I asked one of my sons to put you to music…I'm even envisioning a tv series---"Lester and Estelle."

   Lester, you can direct me anytime…but Lester…will you write for me?

   With great admiration, I am

                            Your devotee

                            Estelle Harris

Steve Wynn with Dolly Parton (above) and with Frank Sinatra disguised as Groucho Mark (below). From a 1981 calendar produced by Wynn's Casinos.
Commercial distribution rights held by Lester Colodny.

A cartoon of Lester flying a magic carpet at The Taj Mahal.

Liz and Lester at their wedding in 1985.

And the President said, "I'm proud to know anyone who knows Lester Colodny."

Roy Gerber with Ronald Reagan

Friends for life: Lester and Leonard Grainger

Advertising Copy, Copy, Copy - 1969

I took stock. A whole year of writing a play with Joan Rivers, producing a pilot, doing a thirteen-week series, and nothing to show for it except a depleted bank balance and not an idea in the world what I was going to do this day, tomorrow or the day afterwards.

But there was unemployment insurance. Yes. I would call and find out where the nearest office was. Where could I find a phone booth? One that still had a yellow pages book with the addresses of government agencies? There were plenty of phone booths. But no phones. They were all either ripped out or had no receivers.

No phones. And certainly no phone books. There was a lot of graffiti. I searched for a store with a phone book.

There was a can in front of me. I kicked it. I kicked it again. Suddenly the can came back to me. I looked up. There was a lovely girl, about thirty-five, blonde, great legs, and a marvelous smile. Smiling at me.

I smiled back.

She said, "Aren't you Lester Colodny?"

"If you have an idea for a play, no."

"Don't you remember me? Lois Korey?" The name rang a bell but I couldn't connect.

"I used to be Lois Balk before I had my nose fixed."

Bingo. "I remember you," I said. "You were one of my young writers at NBC who I slaved to get a job for and never heard from you again."

"That's me. So, Mr.Colodny, the great play writer. I'll buy you a cup of coffee and you'll tell me all about your great writing success."

We sat down at a table outside at Untermeyer's. She said, "I saw your play the other night."

"Uh-oh. I know I shouldn't ask, but what did you think?" I asked.

"The truth?" She said.

"The truth."

"The absolute truth?"

"Yes."

"It stunk."

"That bad, huh?" I said.

"The odor has permeated the entire neighborhood from West Forty-First to the river."

"I know. It closed last night."

"Joan Rivers?" She prodded me.

"No. It was me. My fault. Of course I have to put some of the onus on Alexander Cohen, the great producer's idea. It was his brilliant notion to open it in New York."

"Didn't you have anything to say?"

"Yeah, but I was outvoted. Three to one. Alexander Cohen, her manager and her."

"You should've thrown a bomb. Two bombs."

"Two bombs don't make a right," I quipped sadly.

"That's kind of cute."

"There were hundreds of bon mots like that in the show."

"But no one noticed."

"Not the audience."

"Married?" she queried.

"Divorced," I answered.

"Want to have an affair?"

"Are you suggesting or are you ready for an answer?"

"It was just a thought."

"And you, Lois? What are you doing these days?"

"Bumping into old bosses and making indecent offers."

"I meant what are you doing to feed and clothe yourself?"

"Oh, I'm one of the creative heads at an advertising agency."

"No kidding?"

A waiter came by. "I'm your waiter, Patrick. Can I help you?"

"Two coffees."

"One with strychnine," I said. The waiter made a moue and left.

I asked Lois, "What does a creative head of an advertising agency do?"

"I make up stuff."

"What do you make up?"

"Stuff. To sell other stuff."

"Commercials?"

"And ads."

"I think I see."

"Listen, Lester, let's get serious. What are you going to do now that this show has closed?"

"Damned if I know," I said.

"Would you like to try copy writing?"

"I don't know a thing about it."

"Would you like to try?"

"What have I got to lose?"

She dropped a five-dollar bill on the table, grabbed my hand and dragged me down Third Avenue to Needham Harper and Steers, where she introduced me to her superior, Barry Biederman. "Lester is one of the best writers you never heard of," she told him. "And he's looking."

"Really? What has he written? I mean, what have you written?"

"Tell him," Lois said.

"I just finished—or was just finished by—*Fun City*."

"The play that closed last night?"

"I didn't think anyone noticed."

"And you would like a job writing advertising?"

"It was Lois' idea."

"Well, I'd like to hire you but aren't you a comedy writer?"

"Have you read my notices?"

"Touché. How would three hundred a week be until I find out if you can spell Xerox?"

How does one tell a success story without being thought of as an egocentric boor?

But it all came true. The recognition, the acceptance, the fabulous wife...and the money (not necessarily in that order).

I took to advertising copy (and it took to me) like, if you'll pardon the cliché, a duck to water. After all those years, trying to write screenplays, television scripts, and radio dramas, my typewriter (no computers yet) seemed to spill out copy. Copy that was read. Copy that sold.

I suppose my early training in the composing of précis had much to do with my good fortune. And the agency's.

But all my creative director had to do was hand me an assignment and presto, zappo, within minutes, there was an ad, or a commercial, that was bright, funny, interesting, informative and a sure-fire seller.

I had made the trip to bountiful. I had gone from frustration to fulfillment. How could anyone be so lucky?

My copy won five CLIOS (the advertising equivalent to the Oscars), a dozen Advertising Age awards, countless Art Directors' Club cups, the *Fortune Magazine* Best Writer of the Year, seven consecutive years for my Xerox ads.

I was promoted to group head and then to Executive Vice President.

And I met Liz.

Xerox

After a time, I was put on the Xerox account permanently. I had a fabulous relationship with Wally Olesen who was a vice president of advertising there. Besides being a hell of a nice guy, he absolutely loved everything I created.

From ads in periodicals and newspapers to full color ads in national magazines and television commercials, I was making a name for myself. Wally was my Corporate Godfather.

If anyone questioned an ad or a PR release, Wally was there defending it, saying and proving that my work was enhancing the Xerox brand and image around the world.

I, in turn, got to win multiple awards from newspapers, magazines and industry professionals, which of course means Xerox won them.

It was a match made in heaven.

What a contrast to life in Hollywood.

Some years later the company decided to make their Xerox Learning System's PSS II - a salesman's dream come true - into a new concept: a feature length industrial film. Wally immediately declared, "Let Lester do it."

I'd never made a feature film before. The Jerry Lewis screenplay was a whole different animal. As well as a colossal failure. So when I took on this assignment, both writing and producing, it was with a great deal of angst and trepidation.

I put aside everything I was working on and designed a script that was a total departure from what was then called an Industrial Film. I was not only going to write, but I was going to produce and cast a mini-movie. And I was going it get to do it My Way.

This was not going to be your typical blah-blah-blah instructional film, and I wasn't going to shoot a bunch of boring talking heads. Instead, I was going to inspire, teach, entertain and leave them falling in the aisles.

It was going to take a major investment in time and money, and I was spending both very cautiously. I took a lot of time and care to find just the right actors.

The casting sessions were long and tedious, but I finally came up with three performers to play the principal roles that set the production on fire.

The first was Joe Silver. Joe was a veteran comedy actor who played in every theatrical forum from *Waiting for Godot* to *Guys and Dolls*. He was to play a typical customer, someone reluctant even to think about using something as technical as a Xerox machine.

For Joe's son, among hundreds of actors, we used a then unknown young actor named Richard Dreyfuss. Everybody knows Richard's movie credits, but there is also an interesting Six Degrees of Separation connection. He appeared in Paul Mazursky's film, *Down and Out in Beverly Hills*, he played opposite Barbra Streisand in *Nuts*, and he was in the recreation/adaptation of Neil Simon's play *Lost in Yonkers*.

The hardest part to fill was that of the typical Xerox salesman. A man (it was still pretty chauvinistic then) who would overcome all objections to the Xerox Learning System's PSS II and sell them in quantities to fill railway cars from coast to coast. Hundreds of actors were auditioned.

Then I singled out a young man by the name of Ted Danson. Ted, who happens to be only two months to the day older than Richard, later led the cast of *Cheers* to years of royalties and reruns.

They both came to be considered among the finest actors in television and motion pictures.

The movie was shot at the Xerox facility near Washington, D.C. Unlike the usual quickie Industrial Film, this took months to make. It was exhausting, backbreaking, and a blast. We worked twenty hour days. Every scene was shot, analyzed and reshot to make the comedy work with the sales lessons.

Finally, the day came to unveil the film to Xerox executives and employees from all over the country. They descended on New York's finest premier theatre for the first showing. The audience howled from the opening shot to the final frame and it was a wonderful success.

Not only was the picture a scream, but it actually taught Xerox salesmen how to turn the hardest and most stubborn technophobes into customers. The film was so successful that the company began to market it to other industries. Ultimately, it became one of the biggest-selling sales films ever. And, as far as I know, it was the first professional industrial teaching film to use professional comedy performances.

Wally was exultant. He paraded me around the Xerox centers at Rochester, New York and Stamford, Connecticut as if I were his beloved son who'd simultaneously just won both a Fulbright Scholarship and a Pulitzer Prize.

I was doing a job I was good at, I was getting awards and recognition for my efforts *and* being paid for it. What could possibly be better?

Sheriff Liz

Wally Olesen was my conduit to the Xerox corporation. That he loved my work was evident when one night at his home in Westport, Connecticut, he said to me, "Lester, I want you to stay here at my place while I'm gone. You need a vacation. You deserve it."

I was overcome. In those days folks did not just leave their houses and personal belongings for friends and fellow workers to loll around in.

It was a rare gift and a tribute to the months of work I'd put in. And I was delighted to house-sit.

But before leaving with his wife Candace on their European trip, Wally secretly called an old friend, one Brenda Brody, who also lived in Westport and who knew just about everyone in town.

He said to her confidentially, "Brenda, you remember Lester Colodny, don't you?"

"Yes, he's that super writer you have on the Xerox account."

"Well, he's house-sitting for Candace and me and I want to surprise him while we're away. I mean really surprise him. He's single and you know every single lady in town. Now, I want you to introduce him to some fantastic girls. But can you think of some way to do it that he'll remember for a long, long time?"

"Leave it to me," said Brenda.

She scoured her address book and came up with seven single women and told them what she wanted them to do. A gag was always worth the challenge.

With a drink in my hand, I lay in Wally's easy chair and looked out the window, admiring the trees, the shrubbery, the quiet, rustic charm of the house.

It was absolutely delicious.

On the way out, Wally had said, "The freezer is full of goodies, you don't even have to go shopping. There's plenty of booze, beer and wine in the fridge, and whatever you want for sandwiches. The place is yours for four weeks. Enjoy."

"Go already, you'll miss the plane," I had said.

Wally and his wife Candace left and I got up and wandered around outside, smelling the flowers. I turned on their radio and sat on their patio, feeling like a king surveying his kingdom.

After a while, I went inside, stripped off my shirt and trousers, and stretched like a big lazy, very satisfied cat. What a friend I had. What a house they had. What a great idea this was. I was ecstatic.

Falling into an easy chair, I clicked on the television. There was a ball game on and I half-watched, lazily sipping a vodka and tonic with a sliver of lime.

As I got up for a refresher, I heard a knock at the door. Without thinking about my state of undress, I answered it.

There, standing in the doorway, was a woman in a sheriff's uniform, with a badge and a gun. "Okay, buster," she said testily, "turn around and put your hands against the wall."

"I can explain—" I started to say.

"Quiet," she commanded.

"Wait a second, you don't understand—" I said.

"You do not belong in this house," the sheriff, or whatever she was, said. "We've had calls from two neighbors. They said this place is supposed to be unoccupied for a month."

"No, yes, I mean. Wait. I'm the, what do you call it?" I was so nervous I couldn't even talk. "I'm house-sitting. The owner of the house is on a round-the-world tour," I finally said plaintively.

"Sure he is," she said (with authority). "Turn around and put your hands against the wall."

I put my hands against the wall and she started to pat me down. I was in my underwear shorts and there wasn't much to pat down.

"Wait a minute," I said. "I can prove that I belong in this house."

I rushed into the kitchen to get the directions for using the washing machine and dryer that Candace had written for me but I couldn't find them. Now I was in a panic.

"I'm not going to tell you again," the officer said. "Hands against the wall."

It was then that she touched me. Lightly. Around the groin.

"I beg your pardon," I said.

"Yes?"

"What are you doing? I mean don't you think that you're being a little, well, you know?" I said.

"I don't know what you mean, sir."

"Well, I mean how can you explain what you're doing, after all—"

She said, "Numb nuts. I'm your blind date."

Slowly, I turned around and stared at her.

She said, "Put on your pants, make me a gin and tonic and shut off that stupid television. By the way," she said, "my name is Liz."

Four hours later, after a lot of laughs, conversation and vodka and tonics, she told me that Brenda Brody, who was a pal of the Olsens, had arranged for a different friend to show up at Wally's every night that week.

I said, "Do you have Brenda's number?"

She fished it out of a pocket.

I picked up the phone and dialed. It was close to midnight.

Brenda answered and I said, "Brenda, this is Lester Colodny. Don't send any more girls. I'm keeping this one."

Bulgaria is Just East of the Iron Curtain

Success with Xerox meant that I was one of the writers who wrote and produced any number of commercials that Xerox bankrolled, all over the country and the world.

We shot a traffic commercial in California, one for migrant workers in Florida, and one in the Grand Canyon where the Havasupai Indians were using a Xerox copier for their tribal newspaper.

We made funny commercials on an island off Florida with a shipwrecked sailor who saved his Xerox copier and was putting copies of "help" in bottles and sending them out to sea.

We made commercials in Paris with Marcel Marceau, in London with a cab driver, and in Venice with two men in a gondola, delivering a Xerox copier.

One day, one of the executives at Xerox told us that Xerox, the company, wanted to expand beyond the Iron Curtain. Jeff Cohen, a young art director, and I came up with an idea that took us to Bulgaria. We wrote and storyboarded, frame by frame, a ninety second commercial in no time.

The commercial was highly visual. My way of saying you sort of had to see it to appreciate it.

We had three days to shoot the entire thing. Trust me when I tell you that is a challenge times five hundred. So we proceeded to Sofia, where we met up with an international producer who not only spoke Bulgarian but who knew (and hired) every crack sound and lighting technician on the continent. We set up headquarters in a local hotel and immediately began casting for the commercial.

On the set, even with the language barrier, we all found a way to communicate.

Everybody worked hard and we got it done. The commercial was "in the can" and on its way back to Paris.

Now, I figure you've already figured out that there were "ways" of doing business in those days. During the Cold War in Bulgaria, with Bulgarian officials. It was a tricky business, highly circuitous. With cash, one had to be careful. But we pulled it off and our new best friends, the Bulgarian officials (who shall remain anonymous), decided to fête our crew at a grand luncheon.

As we had already discovered, Bulgaria was full of interesting contradictions. For instance, there was a particular restaurant, famed throughout the country for its superior cuisine, and our hosts were eager to make us aware of what a privilege dining there would be. Great, I thought. I'd like to see some more of city life in Bulgaria.

Instead, we drove out to a tiny little town of perhaps a hundred souls. The lovely quaint inn was straight out of the movies, except this was the real deal. It had the patina of hundreds of years of feet treading cobblestone, ancient rafters and an ambiance of incredible antiquity.

Who knew how many villagers, for how many centuries, had stopped here to rest and refresh themselves. Maybe the early union of the Slavic tribes in 681 had been negotiated at this very spot. It was delightful.

We ate, we drank, and we toasted everything—the shoot, the officials, history, the writers, the lighting men, Bulgaria, the sound men,

Vasil Levski, the national hero of Bulgaria, the producer, the restaurant, everyone and everything. I wanted to give the Bulgarian officials the group photo we had taken of them and the crew on the set, so I went out to the car.

I couldn't believe my eyes. Sitting there was a Chevrolet station wagon with New York plates. There was no one in the car.

I went back inside and looked around. We were the only people in the place.

I told everybody what I had seen, wrote something on a piece of paper, and had one of the waiters sneak out to the car and put it under the windshield wiper of the Chevy.

I wouldn't tell anybody what I wrote.

We all waited and watched out the windows of the restaurant.

A short while later, a young couple came out of the rest rooms that were located on the side of the restaurant and got into the station wagon.

The driver reached out to retrieve the piece of paper that I had written on. He read it and started to howl with laughter. Then he showed it to his female companion and she started to scream.

They looked all around but we all focused on our plates and looked for all the world like innocent diners.

Finally, they drove off still giggling.

When they had gone, everyone wanted to know what I wrote.

I told them. "Schmuck, I told you to make a *left* at Howard Johnson's."

Can you Wynn in Vegas?

One Sunday morning, as I was preparing to go out and play golf with a few friends, the phone rang and Liz answered it.

"Hello. . .yes, just a moment. Lester, there's a Steve Wynn on the phone."

"Who?"

"Wynn. He says he has to talk to you."

"I have about ten minutes to meet the guys and the club is fifteen minutes away."

"He insists on talking to you."

"Jesus. All right."

I picked up the phone. (Liz was on the extension in the next room, listening.)

"Lester Colodny?"

"Yes. Talk fast, I have a golf game."

"My name is Wynn. I own the Golden Nugget Hotel Casino. In Las Vegas."

"Yes."

"I've seen all your commercials for Xerox. I love them. I want you to do the same things for my casino."

"You've seen all my commercials?"

"Yeah. I asked a friend of mine to find out who did those commercials and he told me you did them and I want you."

"You liked them?"

"I loved them."

"So what do you want from me?"

"Will you come out to Las Vegas to talk?"

"About what?"

"Advertising. I'll send a plane for you."

"You'll send a plane?"

"My jet will pick you up at Teterborough Airport. Come in jeans."

Liz appeared in the doorway, her hand pressed tightly over the phone. She mouthed the words, "Holy shit!"

I covered the phone with my hand and whispered, "Let's go. You can go shopping."

"When do we leave?" she whispered.

"When do we leave, Mr. Wynn? Tonight?"

"The plane is on its way now. It will be there by three."

"Okay," I said. "We'll come. . .About three o'clock? Fine."

"How do you like that? He loves all my commercials," I said.

"Lester! By three? But what will I wear?"

"Huh?"

"Oh for heaven's sake," she said. "It's a private jet, Las Vegas, what am I going to wear?"

"He said we should come in jeans."

"Lester," Liz sniffed. "You know I don't even go to the bathroom in jeans."

That afternoon, we boarded a jet and were transported to Las Vegas. A limo picked us up at the airport and drove us to an enormous home in the suburbs of Las Vegas. At the front door, a maid told us to go out to the back yard. Mr. Wynn was waiting.

It was some back yard. More like a football field with a sumptuous patio and an even more sumptuous house.

A tall, very attractive man, about thirty-five, wearing a Mickey Mouse shirt, came out of the house with a big grin on his face. "Hi. I'm Steve Wynn."

I introduced Liz and after some small talk, I said, "I have to tell you, Mr. Wynn. I'm flattered that you like my stuff so much but I have a pretty good job. Why don't you work with the agency?"

"I don't want the agency. I want you. Nobody writes like you."

He knew how to get to me. After only five minutes, he knew. I said, "I don't know."

"How much do you make? Whatever they pay you, I'll double your salary."

I glanced at Liz. She smiled and shrugged. "Double?" I said.

"Plus expenses. And we'll pay to move you out here. What do you say?"

I said, "I'll think about it."

And I did. I wrote pro and con lists. I agonized. We debated.

"Listen, Colodny," Liz said, "the word 'double' is not such a small word."

"Double, shmouble," I countered. "I've got a great job at the agency. My friends are all here. I like it here in New York."

Liz said, "Did you see the size of that lawn? The house? What about zipping around the country in a private jet? You're from Brooklyn and want to be a big shot funny man? What about that?"

"Hmm," was all I could come up with in response.

She pressed her advantage. "Think about it, Lester. New worlds to conquer. You'll be calling the shots, you'll be on top of the heap."

I was starting to falter. "But my world is here, I've been at this agency for five years. Five very happy, award-winning years."

She pulled out the big guns.

"Lester, this guy is something special. He is so charismatic. Hypnotic. He charmed the hell out of you. He believes everything he says. He dreams big. He is determined to be somebody special."

She could see I was floundering.

"Liz, what do I do?"

"We've been all around this. You can't have your cake and eat it too, so just make up your mind and let's get on with it."

There it was. The proverbial light bulb. Just like in the cartoons. But this one was blinking madly, like chase lights on a casino marquis.

Lester Colodny was about to defy one of the oldest maxims on the planet.

I not only was going to have my cake (that I would be dining on at every opportunity), I was about to devour it. I called Barry Biederman, Creative Head of the agency and told him what was up.

Barry said, "You can't do that, Lester. You can't leave. We, we have a great rapport here, fantastic clients, I thought you were happy here."

It was then that I reassured Barry.

"I'm so happy here that I'm not taking the offer. In fact, I'm not only staying but I'm going to bring in a big, fat new account."

Biederman was a happy man.

"I'm not even going to ask you to match Wynn's offer," I said.

The next day, I called Steve.

"Well," Steve asked. "what's your decision?"

I said, "Why don't you come with the agency?"

"I don't want the agency. I want you."

I explained that one didn't come without the other.

We talked, we negotiated, we parlayed and finally Steve gave in. I was exhilarated. On top of Everest. I was having my cake with a vintage Dom Pérignon.

A week later, the agency sent Steve the papers and the Hotel and Casino became a client of the agency. In addition to my regular work at the agency, I took on all the advertising for the Hotel. I did ads, billboards, posters, everything and anything.

However, despite his initial charm, Steve Wynn was not an easy man to work with.

New York account executives are a tough bunch. Especially Sarah Evans, who was the account manager on the Wynn account. Backbones forged in the crucible of cutthroat competition and ego-crazy clients, they're used to being yelled at, they know how to mollify idiotic requests, soothe ruffled feathers and maintain a semblance of sanity in what really is an utterly insane business.

Sarah Evans was cast in that mold. So how was it possible that Wynn, who was her client, had her in tears? Every day. He made terrible demands of her. Impossible demands. Critiques. Harangues. There was no way she could win.

Finally, I had to put in a phone call to Steve and tell him to take it easy on her.

"It's not her," Steve complained. "I'm happy with the advertising but very unhappy with the company I signed with."

About this time, Alan Kay, an art director and I came up with a slogan for the hotel: "We're Going to Make Las Vegas Famous."

The hotel was a small, downtown casino, with three shops across the street from the front door: a liquor store, a pornographic magazine store and a pawnbroker. It was a charming, picturesque place, designed in the old-west style, with two restaurants and a small show room, but nothing more.

I said, "What an idea. We'll shake up the town."

Together with an art director I put several ads together. Full page. Each one with a headline or a kicker, "We're Going to Make Las Vegas Famous." One lauded the desserts by the Chinese chef, another the down-home entertainment in the tiny showroom, still another the warm, fuzzy, loving care that people felt when they stayed at the hotel.

Steve Wynn called me. "What the hell are you thinking of?" he demanded.

I said, "We'll just run them in the local papers."

A week later Steve called me. "I went to a hotel owners' meeting and everyone laughed at me," he said.

I didn't reply.

"They thought I was out of my mind," Steve said.

I stayed silent.

There was a long pause.

Then Steve said, "But they all noticed it. Every one of them. Caesar's Palace, The Sands, every single one of them. Especially the big joints on the strip. I love it. I absolutely looooove it."

For the first time in its history, everyone in Las Vegas was noticing that little hotel with the pawn shop out front.

A couple of weeks later, Steve called me. "Come out. I'm sending a plane for you."

Off we went to Las Vegas. Steve met us at the airport. He embraced me, hugged Liz, and in the limo going back from the plane told us that business had quintupled since the ads had run. We got to the hotel and walked in.

There were people in front of every slot machine. The craps tables were three deep with players. The blackjack tables had black chips (worth a hundred dollars) on them. Even the roulette tables and big wheel were filled.

Steve turned to us. "I just wanted you to see for yourself, Mr. and Mrs. Colodny," he crowed. "Lester, you are a genius."

Genius is good. Great even. But the degree of admiration Steve had for me was defined by its polar opposite in terms of the agency I worked for. He hated it. Despised it. Reviled it.

I don't know why. I can't really explain it. Maybe it was because he harbored resentment about being forced to work with them, instead of succeeding in wooing me away.

We went home and the president of the agency called me into his office.

"Lester," he said, "we have to. . .to get rid of that maniac Steve Wynn. He's driving our staff crazy."

"You mean fire him?" I asked incredulously. In those days, no one fired a client. Ever. It was unheard of.

"I'm afraid so," was the response.

The next day, I was on a plane to Las Vegas. In Steve Wynn's backyard, I explained that the agency and he were not exactly getting along.

"Good," Steve exclaimed. "Now, let's get to it. I want you." We made a deal. I was to become a consultant. I would continue to work for the agency but I would be exclusive to the hotel for casino advertising.

For the next two years, the place flourished. From a small, downtown joint, the casino became a place where the most sophisticated gamblers had to visit, at least once, when they came to town. Business kept increasing. The hotel occupancy was ninety-nine percent. Steve Wynn was in heaven.

I created a billboard and placed it fifty miles out of town. It had a photo of the casino on it. The words read: "Slow Down, We'll Wait." It was a sensation.

The ads and radio commercials, which were outrageous, irreverent, and funny, were the talk of the west.

Steve Wynn urged me, begged me, to become a member of his family of employees.

We were driving to La Jolla, California, Steve, his wife, Liz and I, to talk with an architect who would redesign the place into a modern, up-to-date hotel. On the way, Steve hopped out to get us sandwiches. As soon as he got out of the car, Mrs. Wynn said, "Lester, don't do it."

"Do what?" I asked.

"Do not, under any circumstances, sign with the hotel as an employee."

"But he offered me double my salary and fifty thousand shares of stock," I protested.

"Lester, listen to me. Today you are the girl of the hour. You are a hero. Steve loves you. But the minute, the second, you sign a piece of paper making you an employee, you will become yesterday's bimbo. Please, listen to me."

She turned to Liz. "Please, make him listen."

Liz said she would try.

But I didn't listen. I left my job at the agency and went to work for Steve Wynn. And I must say, the world became my oyster. As much as the agency had been a pleasure, the casino was a blast. Everything I wrote was an immediate success. Success? It was intoxicating.

In a world of writers in New York, I was one of the many up and coming. In a world like Las Vegas, I was a comet shining in the universe. And life with Steve was a ball. He was funny, bright, charming.

Every night, I would come home with stories about how the two of us exchanged quips, questions, puzzles. Steve was a crackerjack on Broadway musicals and he would call me out of the blue and ask me, for instance, who played such and such in the musical whatsis?

I wasn't completely naive. I was familiar with ego-crazed luminaries. Some were worth the bother, most weren't. It's part of being a big shot, I told Liz. When everybody you see, meet or talk to kisses your virtual ass, you start to believe it. The same way you feel like garbage when everybody tells you that you stink.

Neither one is necessarily true, but this is the United States and we rule by majority. So you take that human paradox, and you multiply it by ten thousand, you end up with moguls and maniacs. I ended up with a maniacal mogul.

Yes, I knew Steve was eccentric from the first week I worked for him. I was aware there might be some, shall we say, issues. Because Steve had come up to me and said, "I'm gonna buy shoes. You wanna come with me?"

"I have an awful lot of stuff I should be getting together for you," I said.

"You'll do it later. Come." We got into Steve's limousine. "We're going to Fine Shoes," he told the driver.

"So? How do you like working for a single client?" asked Steve.

"It's been less than a week. So far, I like it a lot."

"If you need shoes, I always get my shoes from the same place."

"I don't need any shoes," I said.

"My father bought shoes from this same guy for years. He's the best. Top quality shoes. That's what I love. Quality. It's why I hired you. Quality. Max Fine sells the best shoes. My father took me there when I was a kid. So how is my advertising coming along? I'm getting antsy for the first ads."

All in the same sentence. While I was pondering what to answer first he said, "I want to hit the newspapers full blast. Two-page ads." Finally. Something I could react to.

I corrected him gently. "Spreads."

"Exactly. Two-page spreads. I want to kick ass, Lester. You know what I mean?"

I nodded. I liked his drive. Then I noticed that we were pulling in to a private airport. The Golden Nugget jet was on the tarmac, warming up, and the stairway was out.

Steve climbed out of the limo and I followed him. Where the hell was Fine Shoes, anyhow?

"Fine Shoes," Steve shouted to the pilot, who replied, "Got it." The pilot shut the door and gunned the jet down the runway.

As we sat back in our seats, I asked, "Where exactly are we going?

"New York."

"New York?" I asked in astonishment.

"Manhattan, lower East side."

From Las Vegas? We were going to New York to buy shoes? Well, I guess it's all relative. I mean, I drive fifty miles to a restaurant I love. I drive. He flies.

"How're you coming with the staff?" Steve asked.

"Don't you think I ought to call my wife and tell her?" I said.

"Nah. We'll be home by dinner time. What about your staff?"

"I'm interviewing people."

A Funny Thing Happened

"Great. Can't wait to see what you put together."

Steve went back to his private bedroom to catch a nap and left me alone to work on some ads that I had thought to bring along. About two hours passed by. I had scribbled up an ad that announced the opening of the spa at the new Golden Nugget Hotel when Steve appeared. He loved it.

Five hours later we were pulling up to a tiny shop, wedged between an A&P supermarket and a Chinese take-out place in lower Manhattan. The sign over the door, reading "Fine Shoes," was chipped and peeling. As we entered, a gnarled gnome of a man rushed to greet us. He grabbed both of Steve's hands and gushed, "Mr. Wynn, I am honored. Please sit. Take your coats off. Would you like a cup of tea, a piece of strudel my wife baked fresh today?"

"Just a pair of black shoes. My regular," said Steve.

"You bet," the little man beamed. "In one shake of a tail I'll have on your feet your favorite shoes I keep in stock. For Mr. Steven Wynn I would stock a thousand pairs of his favorite shoes."

He rushed to the back of the store and returned in two seconds. He wasn't even breathing hard.

He said to me, "Maybe you would like some strudel? My wife baked this with angel's fingers."

"No thank you," I said, patting my stomach. "Must watch the figure."

Mr. Fine shrugged and disappeared.

Mr. Fine reappeared. With a flourish he flipped the lid off the shoe box and displayed a pair of gleaming black loafers. "Voila!" he exclaimed.

They didn't look like shoes that were any different from the shoes they sold in the shop at our hotel but who was I to question?

Mr. Fine helped Steve's left foot into the new left shoe.

"Fits like a glove. Now, the right."

Mr. Fine slid the right shoe on to Steve's foot and subtly winked at me. To Steve, he said, "Walk, Mr. Wynn. Walk like a king."

Steve rose and strode around. "The right is a little tight, Mr. Fine."

"Tight? Tight? Give me two seconds, I'll make perfect."

Steve sat and the little shopkeeper removed the right shoe.

"Tight. Tight is not right," he muttered on his way to the back of the store. "A king doesn't travel all the way from Las Vegas to put on a tight shoe."

"So, when everybody gives double odds," Steve said in a complete non sequitur, "I'll give triple. You have to have an ad ready for that. And when they give away a million in slots, I'll give two million," he added, walking around with one shoe on. "Make sure you have an ad for that too. When it happens, and it will happen, we will not be heard pissing and moaning. Do you know why?"

I shook my head.

"Because the Golden Nugget will already be six jumps ahead of the pack."

"No one can say the king isn't always six jumps ahead of the pack, Mr. Wynn," said Mr. Fine, returning with Steve's right shoe.

He put the shoe on Steve's right foot and Steve admired himself in the mirror. "I'll wear these out. Put it on my bill."

"You got it, Mr. Wynn. It's a pleasure to have you in my shop. Always. And by the way, for later." He handed Steve a paper sack. "I wrapped up, together with your old shoes, a piece of my wife's strudel. Enjoy."

When Steve left I asked Mr. Fine, "How does Mr. Wynn pay you, by check or by credit card?

"Oh his credit, it's good here anytime."

"Mr. Fine, did anyone ever try to sell you a bridge?"

"Sure."

"Did you buy?"

"What do I look like, a schmuck?"

Outside the store, Steve said, "I hate strudel," and handed me the paper bag.

"I'm on a diet, thanks," I said and handed it back.

I took a deep breath. "Mr. Wynn—"

"Lester, you just have to stop that. My name is Steve."

"Steve, there is something I need to tell you about and I'm afraid you may find it upsetting."

"Doubtful," he said, "But go ahead."

"Have you seen *Gambling Times* this month?"

"I heard about it," mumbled Steve and opened Mr. Fine's bag of strudel.

"I have it right here," I said, reaching into my coat pocket.

I read, "'Steve Wynn is the subject of public hatred, contempt and ridicule.' And how about this, 'His business tactics are highly offensive.'"

"Where does that guy come off writing stuff like that about me?" demanded Steve, munching on a piece of strudel. "This strudel is delicious."

"I thought you said every knock is a boost?"

"This is great strudel."

I continued reading. "'The best way to describe Steve Wynn's management style is like putting a bunch of venomous spiders in a bottle. Who ever survives gets to play in the game. Until next time. Which is usually tomorrow.'"

"What an idiot," laughed Steve, spraying strudel crumbs all over me. "I have to evaluate people and situations. I have to have a set of standards. It's only common sense. There's a reason I'm a multi-millionaire and that guy, whoever he is, is just a reporter. You have to manipulate the press or they'll manipulate you," he continued. "That's why my advertising has to be the greatest." He paused. "You know, that was really good strudel."

Later that night, Liz asked what I had done all day.

"I went shoe shopping."

"Lester, you hate shopping. Especially for shoes."

"But Liz," I said, "you always say the best shoes are in New York."

"Lester Colodny. You jetted to New York to buy shoes, without me?" she demanded incredulously.

"I apparently participated in a bonding ritual today. Like a secret handshake. No girls allowed." Liz rolled her eyes, pressed the back of her hand to her brow, and fake-staggered out the door.

A Funny Thing Happened

The days flew by and I was in heaven. Everything I wrote was accepted with praise and admiration. Can you imagine? People driving to Las Vegas had to stop at the Nugget just to see what it was like. And we were always filled up. Even on Tuesday nights when all the other hotels were half empty.

My radio spots were funny. With no one to monitor me, I was able to do what I pleased. I assembled a group of great character actors and we made fun commercials that caught people's attention.

In one of them, you heard two voices. A man and his wife. She said, "Look at this place. The Golden Nugget. It's so beautiful. And lit up. Like a thousand lights. It's so marvelous."

And he said, "And this is only the garage."

While all the other hotel casinos were doing straight, hard sell commercials and ads, we had our tongues surgically implanted in our cheeks. The stuff we did was funny, crazy, and unpredictable so that it really stood out among the clutter.

Steve was beside himself with joy.

One day I was summoned to his office. Sitting there were the president and vice president of the hotel with long faces.

"What's wrong?" I said.

"Sit down," said Steve. "All right, Bob, tell Lester what's on your mind."

The president said, "We think the advertising is a joke. We're the laughing stock of the town. We're a gambling place, not a fun house." Steve turned to the vice president. "Arnie, tell Lester what's bothering you."

Arnie said, "Exactly what Bob told you, Lester. I hear the commercials. I see them. I read the ads. What do you think you're doing?"

I glanced over at Steve. He asked, "How has our occupancy been since Lester joined us?"

The president said, "Ninety-nine point five percent."

"And how is our gambling revenue?"

The vice president said, "Up about thirty-six percent."

"This meeting is adjourned," said Steve. The two executives shuffled heavily toward the door. "Lester, stay here."

Steve said to me, "Who was the lead singer and star of the musical that had, 'How Are Things In Glocca Mora?'"

I knew the answer but I was so happy I could have kissed him.

"Tell me. I can't remember."

"You know it, you asshole."

"I think you're the greatest," I said.

An Offer Frank Couldn't Refuse

To make things even juicier, Steve decided to go to Atlantic City and build a brand new Golden Nugget. One that would outshine every other casino hotel in New Jersey.

Steve and the Golden Nugget were becoming a small dynasty. At least a dyn.

One night Steve and I were having dinner. I casually suggested to him that he ought to try to get Frank Sinatra to sing for the Golden Nugget casinos. He looked at me as if I had left my brains on the subway.

"You have to be joshing me," he said.

"Listen to me, Steve," I said. "With the new hotel you will be in the Big Time. Playing with the big boys. You'll have two hotel casinos so you're going to need something to advertise, something that makes sense with gambling. So who's the one performer who is synonymous with gaming? With high stakes playing?"

"Sinatra."

"Right."

"But how am I going to get him?" Steve protested. "Everybody, I mean everybody's after him."

"Make him an offer he can't refuse," I said.

"Like what?"

"Like a piece of the action."

"A piece of the action?"

"That's what I said. But first, offer his lawyer a piece and his agent a piece."

"That's a lot of pieces," said Steve.

"That's a lot of star."

Three weeks later, Steve called me at home at three in the morning. "All right, I gave away the store, but I got you Sinatra. Start writing."

That night, I sat down and wrote the first Sinatra commercial for the Golden Nugget in Las Vegas. We would have to have him shoot it early in the morning while the casino was still relatively empty. We had to. Otherwise we'd have had a hundred thousand spectators clamoring for autographs.

I am standing in the middle of a casino, practically empty of people except for my crew of technicians, lighting men, sound men, grips, a script lady and extras, assembled from six different cities.

Empty, as in almost shut down.

Only two reasons in the world a casino would almost shut down. One was the actual end of the world. The second was Frank Sinatra. My hero.

I, Lester Colodny, am about to make a film (okay, a thirty-second commercial) with. . .Francis Albert Sinatra. The idol of millions. The star of stars. The most famous singer since Caruso.

Sinatra, whose voice wafts me back to memories of magnificent nights with women I have loved, affairs that blossomed and love affairs lost. A man whose lyric tones defined life and love for multiple generations.

I am going to direct Frank Sinatra.

A Funny Thing Happened

Through my exhaustion I can feel the excitement build as my heart rate begins to crank up. It's 7:30 in the morning and we're good to go.

For days and nights, the crew and I have worked feverishly, using a stand-in, to create a scenario that will enchant the world and make multitudes of people beat a path to these Golden Mousetraps.

And after almost a hundred hours of preparation we are waiting for that breathless moment when he appears.

My God. Me directing the man who made every memory I have. Memories that make me want to weep. Memories that elate me.

He isn't just Frank Sinatra. He is a hundred recollections, a thousand reminiscences, he is a piece, no, a part of my life. A kid from Brooklyn is about to work with the greatest star in the world. I am overcome. It is too much. I have to sit down and take deep breaths.

But. . .there is no Frank Sinatra.

The crew looks at me expectantly. I look back at them and shrug a little sheepishly. Time passes. Finally, I send a couple of assistants out to search for him and one reports back that Mr. Sinatra is "losing his ass at baccarat."

Two hours later, Mr. Sinatra deigns to show up, eighty thousand dollars in the hole. He just stands there. The silence is palpable.

I say, "Morning, Mr. Sinatra. We're ready for your first take. Make-up."

A make-up lady, her fingers trembling, starts to brush Frank's face.

"I don't need none of that shit. Let's do the fucking thing," he grumbles. (None of that shit? Let's do the fucking thing? My main man in the universe has said, "Let's do the fucking thing?" No. I am wrong. Must be the fatigue setting in.)

I turn to the crew. "Let's do it," I say.

The commercial is to be shot in one long take. Thirty seconds long. "Ready, Mr. Sinatra?"

"Yeah," says Frank sullenly. (Yeah? He said, "Yeah?")

The camera man says, "Camera." The sound man says, "Sound." I say, softly, "Action."

And I watch as Frank Sinatra completely botches the take.

"Cut," I say quietly.

One of Frank's bodyguards rushes over and hands Frank a drink and a lit cigarette.

I approach them. "Mr. Sinatra—?" I begin.

"Yeah?" he says.

"We'd appreciate it if you did the commercial the way it was written," I say.

"Whoever wrote that, it was shit," comes out of the mouth of the most famous man in the entire world. In the universe. (Shit? Did he say shit? I must not have heard him correctly.)

I say, "I wrote the commercial, Mr. Sinatra."

"Well, you heard me. It stinks." (Stinks? It stinks?)

"That's the copy," I say.

"Well, it's rotten." (Did he say. . .? No. I must not have. . . rotten?)

"Awright, let's do it and get the fuck outta here," he says. (Get the fuck outta here? My first commercial with Francis Albert Sinatra and he wants to "get the fuck outta here?")

I am shaken to my core.

I say, "All right everybody Let's do it again."

But my star, my hero, my idol, is sitting and bullshitting with his pals. He is smoking. And drinking. (At eight in the morning?)

I say to the star, "Excuse me, Mr. Sinatra, but I'm afraid we can't have any smoking or drinking in the commercial."

"Why?" demands Frank.

"Because. . .because. . .smoking and drinking is not permitted in a commercial."

"What are you talking about? I see television shows all the time. They smoke and drink in plenty of them," he says. His buddies, his pals, his cronies, all nod.

"They don't permit it," I say gently, "in the commercials. They permit it in the body of the shows that the commercials surround."

"What did he say?" says Francis Albert.

I say patiently, "There is a ban on smoking and drinking in commercials."

"By who?" he asks.

"Who?"

"That's what I said, you deaf? Who?"

I am beginning to get just a little tired of explaining things to my idol.

"Mr. Sinatra," I said, "I don't know who. I just know that—"

"Whatever," Frank cuts me off. He drops the cigarette on the rug (that cost the owner of the Golden Nugget thousands) and knocks off his drink in one gulp.

"Let's try it again," I say to the crew quickly.

Suddenly I am approached by one of the star's bodyguards. A big man. A very large man. A huge man, in fact. "Dis is it. You heah? One maw time and the man is troo."

"I beg your pardon?" I asked.

The immense man jabs me in the chest with a salami-sized forefinger. "You hoid what I said. One maw and Mr. Sinatra is troo.'" This is a crucial moment. A very crucial moment. Because, if the commercial is not shot in the next take, Mr. Sinatra is "troo."

I take a deep breath and step forward. With my heart pounding, I look up at this giant and jab my finger into his chest and say, "The man is not troo. He is troo when I say he is troo."

Then I turn to the crew and said, "Now. . .let's do it."

"Speed."

"Camera."

"Sound."

I say, "Action."

Mr. Frank Sinatra walks into the commercial, hits his mark, and says his lines. Dreadfully.

"Cut," I yell.

Mr. Sinatra is walking away from the camera.

I intercept the star. "Excuse me, Mr. Sinatra," I say, "But you will have to do it one more time."

After all these years, I am talking to The Man With the Golden Arm and what am I saying? Not, "Can I have your autograph?" Not, "Thank you for all the incredible songs and music."

I am saying, "You'll have to do it one more time."

And he says, very snottily, "I never do more than two takes. If you don't have it in the can, then you don't have no commercial."(He said, "You don't have no commercial." Just like that. "You don't have no commercial." The man who personally orchestrated the JFK balls? The man who was awarded an Oscar for his role as Maggio in *From Here to Eternity*? The man who is the head of the Rat Pack, said "You don't have no commercial?'")

"You crude individual. You, who I thought was the quintessence of sophistication. You unconscionable, unmitigated jerk. You egomaniacal creep," I say to myself.

Aloud I say, "It was thirty five seconds long, sir."

"So?" he says.

"Commercials can only be thirty seconds long."

"Why?"

Why? Why? You insufferable piece of shit, I think.

There is a long, tense, moment.

Then he says, in a voice that is supposed to sound menacing, "Okay, let's get it over wit."

Now, we do the commercial. And Frank Sinatra does the copy on the commercial exactly the way I wrote it. In one take. And then, without even a backward glance, he walks out of the casino followed by his entourage.

"Twenty-nine and a half, on the nose. Perfect," says the script girl. "Jesus, wasn't he absolutely great?"

"Frank was fabulous," says the make-up girl.

"Mr. Sinatra is the quintessential perfectionist," says the owner of the Golden Nugget, appearing from nowhere.

I look at them all. From the lofty CEO to the lowly script girl. Then I shake my head. My dreams and illusions have gone up in smoke. But I have the commercial, in the can.

I look at my watch. It is ten minutes after ten in the morning. I walk out of the casino to the pool.

It is empty of people.

I dive in. Clothes and all.

Strangely enough, a metamorphosis took place after the commercial aired. I guess it's a guy thing.

Maybe it has to do with testosterone, but any boy at school will tell you when you pick a fight with a guy, and the two of you brawl, you come out of it either mortal enemies or best friends. Frank and I had a go at each other. Now, we were pals.

Sinatra became, at least to me, a mensch. A person of value. Often, we ate together (he loved hot dogs and beans as I did), we laughed together (he loved my stories about Garroway) and anguished over the state of the world together.

In the more than fifteen commercials that we did for the Golden Nugget, and several more for the Sands in Atlantic City, he was always cordial and cooperative. He gave me at least three "takes" and sometimes even four or five (I later learned that he never did more than two for any director in films or commercials, ever).

And in his last years, when he no longer could make it past his two shows a night at the Sands in Atlantic City, without the help of a teleprompter or cue cards, he performed his commercials for me with a professionalism, joy and élan that were completely captivating.

So, in the end, he was a star. A fabulous, talented, and unique personality.

I will always be proud to say that Frank Sinatra was my friend.

Leaving the Golden Land

A number of months later, several technicians and I were putting the finishing touches on the second commercial. This one featured Francis Albert and Steve Wynn.

I said, "Let's run it and we'll see what else we can do to make it look great."

Just then, Steve walked in. He plopped down in a seat and said, "Okay, run it."

Steve was doing his impression of David O. Selznick even though he didn't know his ass from his elbow about the art, never mind the technology, of film. Clearly, he was becoming the cliché of a legend in his own mind.

So what? What did I care?

I was busy thinking quite highly of myself at the time. I was making plenty of money. I had an expense account. If he wanted to play producer, fine by me.

I nodded my head at the technicians, "The man says run it. Run it."

The lights went out and the screen lit up with a thirty-second commercial. In the commercial, Steve walked through a simulated suite at the Golden Nugget. It was sheer opulence. He looked directly to camera and said, "I'm Steve Wynn and I run the Golden Nugget Hotel and Casino. We may be downtown, but we're really uptown. Because appearing at our casino is the one and only Frank Sinatra."

At that moment, Sinatra entered with a bell hop carrying his bags. He tipped the bell man. A very big tip. The bellman looked down at the cash in his hand and said, "Thank you, Mr. Sinatra." Then he left, counting the bills.

Steve ran over to Frank. "Hi, Mr. Sinatra, I'm Steve Wynn. I run this place."

Sinatra now looked around, and without missing a beat, took a bill from the roll he had used to tip the bellman. He handed Steve a tip as if he were a head waiter.

"Make sure I get plenty of towels," Frank said, and walked away.

The camera stayed on Steve who looked at the money in his hand, incredulously.

The camera now moved to a close up of Steve. Steve said, "Towels?"

Steve dissolved into a logo and the lights came up.

"It's not bad," said Steve. "Bring up the music at the end. Shorten the sequence with me so that you come up on my face quicker. Too much Frank and not enough of me. See if you can come closer when I do the walk. And give the whole thing more me instead of Frank, and don't forget, a sting at the end."

He walked out. Everyone looked at me in astonishment. Steve was stepping over the line.

My job was to protect my people and the end product. I said to a secretary, "Read it."

"It's not bad. Bring up the music at the end. Shorten the sequence with me so that you come up on my face quicker. Too much Frank and not enough of me. See if you can come closer when I do the walk. And give the whole thing more me instead of Frank and don't forget, a sting at the end."

I took the steno book from the secretary and tossed it into a wastepaper basket.

"It's a wrap." I said. "Let's go home."

I wrote somewhere between forty and fifty radio and television commercials which I also produced and directed. They were a smash. Business doubled, then tripled. Then it broke into the stratosphere. It was like we had hit our own jackpot. And Steve was a co-star in all the commercials. In fact, he started to believe that not only was it his idea to get Sinatra, but that he was a bigger star than Frank.

I didn't care.

Liz and I traveled first class. By jet, by helicopter, by limo. We had our own three-room suites at each hotel. We were living the life.

Besides, Steve was somebody I really admired. Funny, smart, motivated. How often do you get to say that about a guy you work for?

Since Frank there had been other big and popular stars like Kenny Rogers and Willie Nelson. But Frank Sinatra had a special panache. A sheen of sophistication. So what did it matter whose idea it was?

When Sinatra stepped out on a Golden Nugget stage there was magic in the air. A magic like no other.

From a little joint down the strip in Las Vegas, the Nuggets jumped, leaped, across the street into prominence.

Night after night, limos pulled up to the portes-cocheres in Vegas and New Jersey. They discharged the biggest gamblers and the highest rollers in the history of each town.

And when Frank's shows were over, the limits on the tables went from five dollars to fifty to five thousand. You couldn't get near a craps table. Or a blackjack game. The slots were filled with diamond-bedecked women pouring countless dollars into our machines.

And not only was the casino doing fabulously, the staff was getting wealthy. Steve had to go out and buy high-necked tuxedos and plunging-neckline gowns for all the casino help. The tips flowed like wine.

Frank Sinatra was here and we were a hit. A smash hit. It was a bonanza.

What could possibly have made it all go away?

Well, as I mentioned, I wrote, directed and produced a zillion radio and television commercials for the Golden Nugget. I worked with Kenny Rogers, Dean Martin, Dolly Parton, and Paul Anka. They were all lovely people and genuine professionals.

I'm not bragging when I report that every commercial was hugely successful. I had a great time working with all the various stars.

But Wynn's wife was right. He started to really break my balls.

As the months dragged on, the job became more and more untenable. Somehow, I was still managing to make good commercials, but the process was gruesome and the price was becoming prohibitively high.

No amount of money is worth your self esteem. I was getting more and more disgusted with the job and myself. Then it happened. The straw that broke the camel's ass.

There's a reason that adage says "the straw." It doesn't say the two megaton bomb, or a building the size of the Empire State building broke the poor dromedary's back.

It was something light as a feather, the weight of a single, hollow piece of straw. But that last little bit hit the tipping point. Hard.

Seven years is a long time in today's world. That's how long I had been with Steve. I believed in him, I worked tirelessly to make his dreams come true. And yes, I do know that I was paid for it, but it went beyond that. We were friends, colleagues. Ask anybody who isn't on sitting on a financial edge. That relationship is worth more than money.

One day I was in his office, looking out the window and musing out loud about an idea I had for a new spin on the Golden Nugget Casinos. I tend to pace as I muse and ended up standing behind him. As I turned away from the window, I glanced at what was in front of him, on his desk.

No, I wasn't snooping. Not intentionally.

But what I saw made my heart skip a beat.

He had gifted someone, who was a hell of a lot less involved in the successes of the Nuggets, who had been in the picture for a comparative nanosecond, with a shit-load of stock.

No such thing had ever been offered to me.

You might think: ego-headed jerk, what's your problem? But I felt that Steve Wynn's success was quite directly related to my work.

What the hell? We were friends, amigos, buddies.

Do you understand it wasn't the money the stock represented? Who gave a fuck about the money? I'd been disenfranchised, dissed. By a friend I really cared about. Big time.

And that was the harmless-appearing, hollow straw that broke that poor beast's spine.

I left the Golden Nugget, but I also left my relationship with Steve untarnished by recriminations. It was just time to move on. So I did. It was a great ride while it lasted.

I was unemployed, but this time it felt great.

The City, His City

The city had changed.

Turned around.

For better or worse, no one could agree.

Kids out of college were suddenly making half a million bucks a year, driving Porsches and BMWs and buying million dollar co-ops on the east side of New York. Welfare hotels were being swapped and sold for high priced high style condos. A new hot restaurant came into vogue every week. The Big Apple had turned into Ego City USA. Everybody was buying and selling. Everything. Anything.

Even each other.

Almost overnight there were hundreds of limos with dark-tinted windows and uniformed chauffeurs clogging the streets, parked outside of clubs, hotels, restaurants and office buildings.

It was as if half the city's population had given up sleep and the other half had started doing drugs and dry white wines.

No lawyer worth his salt was defending or suing, he was too busy making a billion dollar leveraged buyout of a blue chip company.

Gotham had become Screw 'em.

George Steinbrenner hired and fired Yankee managers like a man with a cold going through a box of Kleenex.

Professional athletes sought out business managers to handle their multimillion dollar endorsements.

Cable TV spread its wings and New Yorkers had fifty-nine stations to watch, including all night news, 24-hour soul-saving and hardcore porn.

The mayor opened his bankbook and started handing out keys to the city to anyone who would put some money where the mayor's mouth was. Tax abatement was an euphemism for "come and get it." And The Man hocked everything, including his mother's wedding ring, to buy property he could build on.

He bought, he optimized, he leased. He built, rebuilt, renovated, refurbished. Every project became a down payment on another. Every building became collateral for two more.

He bought vacant lots, abandoned warehouses, burned-out tenements, empty theaters, bankrupt department stores, lofts, co-ops, condominiums, a bridge, a tunnel, private roads, air rights, easements, rights of way.

From womb to grave and everything in between, if it was for sale at a good price, he was interested. At a better price. For him.

Everybody wanted to just catch a glimpse of the boyish smile, the jaunty step, the cocky stride.

He was the Big Kahuna, the modern day Midas. Everything he bought turned to twenty-four carat gold.

He had the touch, the manner, the confidence and the arrogance. Bankers fawned, financial analysts groveled, vendors trembled at the most fearless, flamboyant and phantasmagoric figure in America.

Maybe the solar system.

You couldn't pick up a newspaper, magazine, turn on a radio or television set without seeing or hearing about him.

Publishers begged for an autobiography. Producers pleaded for a life story mini-series.

He was rumored to be romantically connected with stars, models, anchorwomen, publishers and other men's wives.

He was John Wayne, Ted Williams, J.P. Morgan, Ronald Reagan and a dozen other luminaries all rolled into one.

His limo jammed traffic, his yacht blocked harbors. His private jet flew more miles than Air Force One.

He was number one.

And I, Lester Colodny, was going to be working for him.

The King and the Champion - 1986

I am at one of the buffet tables in the grand ballroom of a magnificent hotel in New York City, along with about eight hundred other people.

Everyone who is anyone in the sports business—reporters, editors, managers, boxers, hangers-on—are all talking, noshing and waiting for The Boss and the heavyweight champion of the world to come in to this press conference.

Actually, everyone is here to meet, greet and pay homage to the proprietor of this hotel and one of the great self-promoters in the world. The Man Who Would Be King.

Except me, naturally. I am just one of his minions, an advertising consultant. And as I speak, I am looking over an array of goodies that would make Julia Childs' mouth water.

The crowd is buzzing but my attention has been drawn to a chopped liver replica of his head complete with smile and hairdo. Even the shape and color of the hair does not dismay me.

As I reach for a cracker and a knife to slice off a piece of the nose, I look up to see a horde of reporters and photographers trying to push cameras, microphones and tape recorders into his face. The reporters are determined to interview His Lordship, His Honor, His Nibs, as he presses into his magnificent gold and velvet ballroom.

The chopped liver nose is wonderful and I move to a piece of curried chicken. It is delicious.

The crowd is now pressing forward to catch a glimpse of His Worship when suddenly there is a hush as the entourage stops. He faces the cameras. The questions come at him, fast and furious:

Why did he buy this famous hotel? Why is he hosting this night for the champ? Does he think he might be a candidate for the presidency someday?

I look around for a waiter. I want a drink. Champagne, Diet Coke, anything. The curried chicken was delicious but left a strange taste in my mouth.

It doesn't matter what he says. He is news.

He senses, smells, feels the power of the press, to everlastingly help him recreate himself in his own image.

I spot pigs in blankets. I love pigs in blankets. I take three. Four.

The crowd buzzes. I look up from my fifth little hot dog and see another group of bodyguards sweeping yet another man into the room. The band strikes up a jubilant melody as the champion, his managers, promoters, followers, and hangers-on enter.

I reach for a small piece of rye bread and some kind of cheese. I taste it. It is an exquisite imported Camembert.

I can see the two men embrace. They smile for the cameras and we toast them.

I don't exactly toast them. I wave my arm looking for a waiter.

I search the table. Ah yes, chopped herring in the form of a giant boxer. Unusual. I take a sample from the right glove. Simply grand.

Reporters shout questions. A cameraman is trampled by the crowd. It is bedlam. It is, of course, glamour and glory and power, by association. By simply being in the presence of these two marvelous, mystical majesties, everyone is anointed.

The two are now on the makeshift stage and The Kingmaker is shushing the crowd and introducing the most brilliant, the most ferocious, the most magnetic fighter of the century. The crowd roars its approval.

I look around for a lemon peel to add zest to the calamari. This table layout should be recognized as an utter gourmet paradise.

Now, the champion steps forward to speak.

But who is that that keeps talking?

I notice rare roast beef on a serving platter. I look for a serving fork. There is none. I gingerly pick the roast beef up with my fingers. So tender, so utterly palate pleasing, a person could die. I take two more slices.

Basking in the glow of adulation and press coverage The Chief is telling the world press how he performed the miracle of putting this press conference together in just two hours. The crowd shouts hosannas. I finally catch the eye of a waiter and order a flute of champagne.

I must say, he is charming, disarming and Mr. Wonderful as the heavyweight champ shadow-boxes around.

"And now, my fellow Americans, I take great pleasure in presenting to you—"

The crowd is stomping and shouting as The Champion steps forward again and says a few words. But no one listens. They are all glued to You-Know-Who. Because the moment, the night, is his.

I taste the champignons. Where did they find such exquisite mushrooms at this time of the year? I fill my plate with them.

As the Champ natters, The Boss meanders over to me and out of the side of his mouth whispers "So, Lester, how'm I doing?"

My mouth is full so I can't answer. Without waiting for an answer, he is gone. I'm thankful.

I carefully remove a mushroom from my mouth and place it discreetly in a napkin. Not all of them were exquisite. I poke around in the nut bowl and find almonds. I simply adore almonds. And here is the waiter with my champagne.

My Leader is so incredibly visible for all the world to see, to admire, to live up to. He is the embodiment of the American dream, this star of stars, builder, real estate owner, and mogul, mover, shaker; bigger, larger than life.

I take a sip. Not bad for domestic.

The champion is still mumbling as The Wonder of the World works the crowd, shaking hands, kissing cheeks, and asking what they think of the press conference. Isn't it marvelous?

Put together in only twenty minutes? Isn't he the most incredible public relations expert? Isn't he the living end? Was there ever anyone, anywhere anything remotely like him?

Mention his name in Sheboygan, San Francisco, New York, Orange, Perth Amboy, Sioux Falls, and everyone knows who he is.

Who cares if the sun shines or the world turns on its axis? As long as there is someone to report on something he says or does or didn't say or didn't do! Where will it all end?

The trays are empty now. The waiters are clearing the empty plates and glasses. I wonder, how did I get mixed up in this? And most of all how will I eat dinner?

I look around for my wife There she is. Beautiful, charming, and elegant. I push through the crowd to greet her.

I get her aside and whisper, "So, Liz? Give me a bird's eye. How did the press conference go?"

She says, "There's a good movie at the Thalia. We can make it if we hurry. And brush those crumbs off your jacket."

How does a person describe HIM? There was and is no other. Thank God.

Egocentric to a fault, absolutely impervious to critique, unabashedly selfish, he was one of a kind. They not only broke the mold after him, they squashed it for all time.

And I worked for him. Three years of my precious existence in the service of an undeniable, unflappable, unappreciative prick.

Three years. Two lifetimes.

How I unconsciously fell into his clutches and miraculously escaped is the horror story of the ages.

It began when I received a telephone call from one Allan Storm, who was the president of his two properties in New Jersey. Allan and I had worked together at the Nuggets casino, where he had been the General Manager.

"How the hell are you?" he asked.

"How should I be?"

"What are you doing these days?"

"Marv Carleton hired me to do the advertising for the new Monument Casino."

"They haven't poured the cement yet," said Allan.

I said, "Please don't raise your voice, someone may hear you."

He laughed. "Lester, I have a proposition for you."

"Tell me."

"Well, I'm the president of two casinos in New Jersey."

"So?"

"I want you to come down and give us a hand."

"To do what?" I asked.

"Our advertising. Somehow, it doesn't have any punch, any lift. It kind of lays there like a lox. I want you to give us some jazz. Like you did with Steve. You know, some humor. Catchy lines. Clever billboards. You know what I mean."

"But I work for your competitor," I said.

"Well, I'll let you in on a secret," he said. "Guess who is going to buy the Monument?"

"No!"

"Yes. The one and only. So, I'll call Marv and ask him if he'll share you with us."

"Okay with me."

Two days later, Allan called. "I spoke with Marv and it's all right with him. When can you start?"

I drove down to Atlantic City. It was as awful as usual. All those gorgeous casinos along the beach and the rest of the city in complete shambles. It was pitiful. Elegant hotels surrounded by a dreadful ghost of a town.

I looked straight ahead through my windshield and drove into the garage of one of His casinos.

Mickey Garagiola greeted me with a big hug and took me around to meet the Vice President of advertising and public relations.

"Got you Lester," Mickey said. "He did all the great Nugget stuff for seven years when I was there. I'm sure you can use his brain."

And he left.

The VP was very gracious.

He showed me around the place, got all the advertising and public relations plans out for me to look at and then said, "What do you think?"

I said, "I think we'd better get to work."

We changed our signs all around the town to humorous, funny slogans. We switched all our messages from "Come On In" to "You Have To Be Crazy To Play Anywhere Else." And before you knew it, people noticed and business started to pick up.

Mickey called me in and offered me a contract. He said, "You did it again." I now had two customers and they were both happy as clams.

For weeks I had been trying to come up with an advertising message that would fit the garage. I had to convince customers who were driving to Atlantic City to ignore the casino garage that was smack dab at the end of the main highway, and go left for a mere hundred yards further into our casino garage.

This was going to be much more difficult than it sounds. Gamblers were impetuous, thoughtless people. All they wanted was to park as close as possible to a casino, sit down in front of a slot machine and throw their money away. And the other casino had the monopoly on their miserable souls.

I called an old friend of mine, Sidney Wollersheim, a producer of a jingle house. "Sid, I have to find a song that has a catchy, be-bopping sound that we can write new lyrics for, to make people do something."

Sid didn't even ask what. He was in the music business. He knew how to make things work.

Two days later, he called. "I think I found it. I found a song that used to be very popular and I think we can probably buy it for bubkiss because the music publishers want to keep it alive. I think we can put lyrics to it that would solve the problem."

Later that day, I went over to his place on Thirteenth Street and listened to a recording of the song. It was very effective. Now all we had to do was write the jingle that would be catchy and make people think. No, not think, act.

That night I wrote the jingle. Now all we needed were the rights to the song. I called Sid and told him to call the publisher of the song and see how much they wanted for it. I crossed my fingers.

He called me back an hour later. "I got the song. For a song."

"Let's make a demo," I said.

That afternoon, with four singers and a piano, drum and bass fiddle accompaniment we made the tape. It was sensational.

I thanked everybody who had contributed and told them to keep their fingers crossed. We might just have a winner. Then I went down to grab a cab up to the Maestro's office.

He was on the telephone when the secretary ushered me in. He was about thirty-five, tall, blond, kind of handsome with a chubby face. He wore a blue suit with a pink shirt and a red tie. I had seen his photos in the papers and on TV a hundred times, but in person he was taller and more dashing.

"Get me the Mayor, Baron Hilton, and then George Steinbrenner," he was saying. "I want a Pritikin tuna salad, a haircut and a manicure. In ten minutes."

The Mayor? Hilton? George Steinbrenner?

He punched another telephone button. "Listen, Levy, I don't give a shit what they're asking for the property. I'm offering a tenth. That's what I said, a tenth. That's it. I'm gonna get that property and fuck him where he sits." He hung up.

"Now, Gelb," he said, addressing a little fat man slumped in front of his desk and totally ignoring me, "how do I look in the press today?" No introductions. No amenities. It was as if I was a phantom in the room.

"You look great. Just great."

"Did you see the *Times*?"

"You're big in the *Times*, very big."

"*The Wall Street Journal*?"

"*The Journal* says you're the king. They practically crowned you. Like royalty. *The Journal* loves you."

Mr. Gelb turned and smiled at me as if we were old friends. I smiled back.

"Yeah, I'm like this with *The Journal*, but those assholes at the *News*—" he said to Mr. Gelb.

Gelb was an Irving the Agreer. Whatever the boss said, he agreed to.

I thought, go get him, Mr. Gelb. I know an expert when I see one.

"And *Newsweek*?"

"Aren't they the biggest crock of crap at *Newsweek*? I ask you." Gelb peeked at me to see if I agreed. I nodded vigorously. Mr. Gelb was happy to have an accomplice in the room.

"*Newsweek* said I was the best," the chief said.

"That's what I said, boss," said Gelb. "They used to be a crock. But lately, they're like a whole new magazine. Great. Just great." Again he smiled at me. He had found an ally.

"But that Sam Donaldson never gives me a break."

Gelb's lips pursed in an exaggerated scowl. "What do you expect from a guy with a three-dollar hairpiece?"

"The man is a world class jerk."

"You said it," Gelb agreed.

Suddenly, The Man stood up and walked toward the window. He looked out at New York. His New York. "The world is full of schmucks," he said. He said it as if the world being full of schmucks was a personal affront to him.

"You bet your life," agreed Gelb. "All schmucks."

Mr. Gelb had finally made it half way up his boss' behind.

"By the dozens. By the millions. Look out there."

He swept his arm at Central Park, the Bronx and Staten Island, too. Gelb looked.

"Schmucks, schmucks, schmucks," the creator of buildings said.

I stole a look. All I could see was traffic.

Then he turned and glared at Gelb. "Except for Barbara."

The expression on Gelb's face transformed from beatitude to earnestness. "Oh, no, not Barbara. She's beautiful. The way she did that one-on-one with you. A whole fifteen-minute segment in your penthouse. Oh no. That Barbara's the best of the best. The absolute best."

Gelb beamed at me. I beamed back.

"Unless she hates you," said The Giver and Taker of All Things.

The expression on Gelb's face transformed again. "Then she's a bitch and watch out. Oh, you'd better watch out if Barbara has you on her shit list. Watch out." Gelb gestured to me that I had better watch out for Barbara, too. I didn't know which Barbara Gelb was talking about, but was I ever warned.

"So, Gelb, what do we have on the nightly news tonight?"

Gelb paled. I figured he was nailed. "I'm not sure. But I'll find out."

"You're not sure? You're not sure? I pay you a lot of money. More than you're worth. You're paid to know whether or not we're on the nightly news. If you don't know, then you're not doing your job and that means I have to go out and find another PR man. Is that what you want me to do, Gelb? Am I on the early news or am I not on the early news?"

I edged toward a window and looked out. I didn't want to see a contender knocked out.

But Mr. Gelb got off the floor. He was game as could be. "I've gotten you on the news every night for two months, practically," said Gelb.

He jabbed. "The early news, the late news, news breaks, Channels Two, Three, Four, Seven, Nine, Eleven, Twelve, PBS. You name it, you're on it."

Gelb was on the ropes but he was punching back. Lefts, rights. "Every paper in the country has feature stories about you. In every country in the world, practically. In Egypt, China, for Christ's sakes. Magazine covers, features, interviews. . ." Gelb was running out of breath.

"Am I on the early news tonight?"

Gelb caved. "I'll find out."

Eight, nine, ten. You're out! The winner and still champ, the world's most famous entrepreneur.

When Gelb was gone he said, "See that Gelb? The finest personal public relations man in the city. Maybe the country."

I couldn't help thinking, if that's what you do with the finest, what do you do with the worst? I decided I didn't want to know.

"Who are you and why are you here?"

"I came to play a tape for you. This will take about sixty seconds of your time."

"All right. Let me hear what you've got."

I crossed to his combination TV and stereo and put the tape on.

The quartet sang the jingle I had written.

When it was over he said, "Play it again."

I rewound the tape and played it.

He said, "Play it again."

I played it once more.

He said, "What's your name?"

"Lester Colodny."

"You are a genius, Mr. Colodny," he said.

I was really flattered. "You like the tape?"

"Like it? It's tremendous. 'The Man from New York City.' Who, I ask you, who is The Man from New York City?"

I realized what he meant. It was him. I said, "You of course."

"Of course. And those lyrics. Did you write them?"

"Yes."

"They're fantastic. Those lyrics say that my hotel casino is the best and that people shouldn't even notice the other one, without even mentioning their garage, and that they should park in mine. It is absolutely incredible."

I had to hand it to him. I would have been explaining the subtext for a week with any other high-end corporate guy. Usually to no avail.

"Sit down."

I sat.

"What do you do around here?"

"I'm an advertising consultant for both of your casinos in Atlantic City."

"Then you work for me?" he said.

"That's right," I said.

"When did I hire you?"

"You didn't. Your CEO in Atlantic City hired me."

"But who do you think signs your checks?"

"I never noticed," I said.

"You know, you're just the kind of man I've been looking for. You're very theatrical. I love theatrical. Do you know I'm surrounded by dull lawyers and accountants? Not an original thought in their heads. I have to come up with all the ideas. Everything is on my shoulders."

I didn't know what to say so I remained silent.

"How would you like to work with me?"

For an instant I was enchanted. To be the associate of this man was—then I caught myself. "Thank you very much. I'm very flattered but I have two big jobs to do already." I got up to go.

"When are we going to play that jingle?" he asked. "I love it."

He had already forgotten his offer to me. Thank the Lord.

"You'll hear it on the radio in about a week."

"Fantastic," he said.

We bought time on all the networks, the jazz shows, the news stations, everywhere that potential slot machine, craps and blackjack players would be likely to hear our song. The influx into the parking garage was enormous. "The Man from New York City" was a hit.

The CEO congratulated me. The Emperor was overjoyed. He sent for me.

"I'm the toast of New York with that commercial," he said. "I want you to come up here and work with me."

I said, "I'm up to my—"

"Forget it. From now on, you're an integral part of my company." He hit the button on his intercom. "Mona. Get an office ready for Lester Colodny."

I called my wife. "Liz," I said, "I have good news and bad news."

"Tell me the good news first."

"The 'Man From New York City' is a sensation. I understand business has tripled since we started playing the commercial."

"Now tell me the bad news."

"He wants me to come to Manhattan to work with him."

"You realize what you're saying?" she said.

"It's his company," I protested.

"You are about to give up the best situation you ever had."

"I don't see how."

"Lester, you dope. It's the same thing you had with Wynn. As long as you were his consultant, you were the girl with the big boobs and the great behind that he had to have. As soon as you signed on with Wynn, what happened?"

"I got lost in his arms."

"You bet. And the same thing is going to happen to you with this guy. Lester, say 'no.' Say anything. But do not go to work with him. He will chew you up and spit you out."

"What if he insists?" I said.

"Some people never learn," she said and hung up.

Who the Hell is Arnie Frick?

I was showing The Man some ideas for his new casino, when he suddenly turned to me and said, "You know, I think you should let Arnie Frick go."

This was strange because there was nothing he liked to do more than dismiss people himself. In fact, he loved to fire people.

But inasmuch as I was into making a nest somewhere in the vicinity of his rear end, I said, "Okay. Whatever. Consider Mr. Frick to be terminated."

I didn't know who the hell Arnie Frick was. But sure as hell, as soon as I found out, he would be a candidate for residency in a Frigidaire carton.

"You should have him thrown out on his ass, the dumb bastard."

"You're right," I said. "You are so right. As of this moment Mr. Frick is as canned as six ounces of tuna."

"You are my most trusted and closest advisor, aren't you, Lester?"

Really? I thought. When did I become your closest and most trusted advisor?

"The answer is," he said, reading my mind, "last night I decided."

Now. Now the moment had arrived. He was going to entrust me with an inside secret.

"You know my business. You read the papers. You watch television."

"I do. I not only watch it, I devour it. You can be certain that I know as much as possible about the business of all of your businesses."

"Good. Then if you know the business of all my business, why didn't you know that Arnie Frick was fucking up my deal behind my back?"

A good question. "To tell the truth," I said, "I knew somebody was screwing up something but I didn't know exactly what it was. But you can be absolutely, positively certain this will be the last thing he craps up for you." That was, as soon as I could find out who Arnie Frick was and what he did.

"Good thinking."

"Yes, sir."

"Excellent."

The man was an enigma. An enigma wrapped into a puzzle. Not to mention a giant pain in the ass. I had to be on my toes at all times. I said, "Is it possible that somebody whispered in your ear that this Arnie Frick was up to no good?"

"What's the difference? Arnie Frick is a piece of shit. No talent. No imagination. And besides, he's a prick."

"So someone, almost as close as I am, has confided in you."

"Yes."

"And you believed them?" I said.

"Why would they lie?"

"Well, did it ever occur to you that someone was trying to make points with you? Maybe manipulate a better deal for himself?"

"Hmmm. Yeah. Everybody always thinks they're smarter than me. They never learn."

I nodded.

"But Lester, I can't let the creep go because he knows too much about my affairs."

"So you can't just zap him?" I said.

"No. But you can. You're my closest and most trusted advisor and I say you can do it."

I said, "Most trusted and closest advisor."

"Right."

"Got it," I said.

"But I just told you, he knows too much about everything I do. So if I blew him off he could go to my competitors. . ."

"Then I can't fire him," I said.

"Right."

"Don't worry. I'll see to it that Mr. Arnie Frick is taken care of properly."

I walked out of his office and leaned against the building as people rushed by. Is that what it was like to be a genius? To go in four directions at the same time and end up before you began?

Of course I could resign. And maybe get a job somewhere else. But not with the amount of money I was making. The money was unbelievable.

And why should I leave? Just because the boss is insane?

The world was full of peculiar individuals. And the fact that they all did business with him, and he with them, had nothing at all to do with anything. Or me.

Let's face it, I said to myself. (Already I was talking to myself. And answering.) Let's look at this entire matter. Straight in the eye.

You, Lester, I said to my reflection in a store window, are not going to make sense of anything that does not make sense. Not now or any time in the future. So forget it.

Go back to the office and take a nap.

Instead, I walked into Garagiola's office and said, "Mickey, who the hell is Arnie Frick?"

"He Arnie Fricked you?" Garagiola cracked up laughing. "There is no such person. Mr. Colodny, I'm afraid you just got fucked by Frick."

How Much Would that Weigh?

Every time I turned around, he had another deal. And another deal meant that someone else was getting one of his treatments. They were being out-maneuvered, surrounded, with their flanks closed off, their escape route blocked, and their supply trains stranded. Because, when it came to money, cold hard cash, he was relentless.

No one, and I mean no one, got the better of him. Ever.

I was sitting in Garagiola's office when he came in, shaking his head in disbelief. "You won't believe this," he said. "You will not believe it."

"What happened?" I asked.

He got up and shut his door and then drew me over to the corner that was furthest from the door.

A man had been hired to build a huge concrete portico for the new Monument casino. It was to front the ocean and was designed almost like an ancient fortress to encircle the entire resort. Tons of concrete were poured into giant molds and slowly but surely the entire structure was built up to its final massive proportions. Then it was adorned with huge figures and images.

The contractor came in and said the job was done. And he presented him with the final bill.

The Man looked it over and said, "This is too much."

"What do you mean, too much? I only charged you five percent over my initial investment. Five percent. I ordinarily charge twenty percent but for you I did it as a favor. Because I knew how much you wanted to make this place fabulous."

"It's still too much."

"Look, we had a deal. Do you realize what this would have cost you if you had gone to anyone else? Do you realize how many tons of concrete went into building that, that, thing? I had to bring in designers from Italy and Greece to make sure that the figurines were authentic looking. I had to—"

The Boss said, "It's too much."

The man was beside himself. "What do you mean, too much?"

"Just what I said. You can charge me, say, one third of the this bill," The Monarch of Fifth Avenue said.

"One third?" exclaimed the contractor. "One third? That's insane, we've been working for months, I'll go broke. I'll be ruined."

"Well, then. If you won't accept a third—you'll just have to take back your cement."

I sat there open-mouthed. "He told the man to take back his cement?" I said in disbelief.

Garagiola said, "I was sitting right there."

On Television

"It's the energy and the brain and the real potential that I love in a man and from the first time, I saw the potential in him. He had a goot head on his shoulders."

I thought, *he had a head but it wasn't on his shoulders.*

The top-rated TV inquisitor ran up and down the aisles winking happily at the audience. She had as her guests the ultimate superpower couple. Today promised thrills for her audience, her sponsors and her network. The ratings would be astronomic.

I sat in the audience and watched. It was bound to be a bloodbath.

Skipping up to the stage and past the color cameras, the hostess sat between the exquisitely coifed wife, in a green suede Scaasi, and the tall, handsome husband, in his trademark Brooks Brothers basic black.

"Columnist Liz Smith of *The New York Post* calls you the Burton and Taylor of today. How does that make you feel?"

Maybe, maybe, you will be civil, today. Hah!

"Vell," replied the better half, "vere is the glamour anymore, these days? Today's movie stars, they are not glamorous like the old stars. Now, they knew how to be and sell vot they had to sell, so today people are looking at new people vich are coming up to glamour and the vay they live and vork and exciting, vit style and it is so special for them."

She has an opinion but I'm be damned if I knew what it was. And who cares anyhow?

The number one interviewer in all of TV looked at the other half and invited his opinion with a wave of her hand.

"I agree," he said.

You agree, or do you really agree?

The audience applauded and shouted. The floor manager signaled that they were going to a commercial break.

In the silence between segments, the woman whose every question lingered on the ears of her listeners gushed, "They love you. Love you. Now, when we come back, I'm going to ask you about your new apartment."

The stage manager flashed five fingers at the toastmistress, then four, three, two, one, and the three of them beamed at the camera with the little red light.

"Now," said the hostess with unabashed excitement, "tell us all about your new triplex apartment."

They were on safe ground, now. For the moment.

"Your taste, I suppose it changes as vun gets more mature and older," opined the elegant millionaire's wife. "And vee appreciate more the old beauty and antiques and paintings. My lover doesn't like modern art."

"I hate modern art," he said. "You know what a modern artist is? A schmuck who throws paint on a canvas."

Did he really have to say that? What the fuck is wrong with him?

The audience hooted, howled and stomped its feet. The Hostess with the Mostest was ecstatic. Every comment would make a great sound bite on the nightly newscasts all over the country.

"We'll take a call from one of our viewers. Go ahead, Melissa Potashnick of Bloomfield, Indiana."

Over the studio public address system, a voice asked, "This question is for the Mister. Do you and Rowena ever argue?"

Here we go. It was odds-on that he would make a putz of himself.

The audience clapped and leaned forward, expectantly.

"We never argue," he said impishly.

How do you like that? But wait.

"Because she does what I tell her to do."

Why do you have to be such a horse's ass?

The audience booed.

"Chauvinistic pig," snarled the downtrodden wife. The audience stood up and cheered.

In the limo, as he made calls, she hunkered down in a corner, seething. I looked out a side window. I was not going to be a part of this fiasco.

"You are a fuck," she hissed.

"What's bugging you? That audience loved us."

"You made me out to be the maid, you shit," she said, staring out the side window.

"Lester," he said, "you saw the show. How did we come off? Was it a quality interview? I ask you. Did we come off as class? Did she come off as a top wife? What do you think, Lester?"

Fuck you, Mr. High and Mighty. You are not going to get me inveigled into this argument, I said to myself. Aloud I said, "Who do you like tonight, the Knicks or the Nets?"

"You are the top," she said furiously. "You are the top of a pile of shit. Let me out here," she shouted to the chauffeur. The limo pulled up to the curb and she stomped out of the car and huffed away.

The odds on a divorce had just gone down to even money.

A Minnow in a Shark Tank

I had dinner with Liz at one of His hotels. I looked around for the sommelier and when I caught his eye I ordered a bottle of red. Imported. I wasn't paying. Just eating and drinking.

I said to her, "Now, where were we?"

"I was telling you that—"

"You know, Liz," I mused, "you look beautiful tonight."

"Don't change the subject."

"I'm just telling you, you're breathtaking in black."

"Lester, what's doing in the altered state of His Majesty?"

"I feel like going back to the suite right now and getting into the Jacuzzi with you. So what do you want to eat?"

"You'll break your back, both your legs and your heart trying to fit into this mold, you know."

"I don't know what you're talking about."

"Yes, you do. This is not who you are."

"I know he's got a unique presentation. But you can't dispute the man's success. He's brilliant. He makes heaps and mounds and mountains of money."

"But at what cost?"

"I don't know. He doesn't pay the going interest rate, he'd never let them get away with charging what they charge everyone else."

"I'm not joking, Lester. If you swim with sharks, you can't be a minnow. You, my dear, are going to be gobbled up and spit out."

"I don't understand."

"I do love you. And I'm not passing judgment. I'm just saying this isn't your style, it's his. And it clearly works for him. But I can smell what's coming."

"What can you smell?"

She threw her hands up.

"Waiter. Menus, please."

"No. I want to know why you feel this way."

She looked at me. "Alright. How did it go today?"

"The same."

"Answer the question."

"Not bad."

"Not bad? It's going to get progressively worse, you know."

"Why must you be so pessimistic?"

"Lester, at the risk of using an old, old expression, money isn't everything."

"I know, but this is stupid money I'm making, Liz. I'm at the top of the biggest heap in America. You have to admit, the view is great."

No answer.

"You haven't a lot of confidence in me," I said.

"Oh, I have confidence, alright. Confidence that at some point in the future, you're going to be living on a diet of humble pie."

Touchas on Tisch

I was sitting and schmoozing with Mickey Garagiola when his secretary came in and announced that there was a Mr. Kellerman outside who wanted to see him.

I got up to go but Mickey said, "No, wait. I want you to hear something. Send him in."

She went out and left the door ajar. Through the door came a small, wizened figure of a man, about sixty or eighty, I couldn't tell. Before he sat down he said, "So, Mr. Garagiola, what's with The Chiseler?"

"God knows. I tried to find your contract, Mr. Kellerman."

"Never mind what God knows, I have a copy of it right here." Mickey started to introduce me but Kellerman waved his hand and slipped a sheaf of papers onto the desk.

Mickey hardly looked them over and handed them back to Mr. Kellerman. "I have bad news, Mr. Kellerman. I don't know how to tell you."

"Tell me."

"Well, the boss says you overcharged him and that he's going to sue you."

"He owes me hundreds of thousands of dollars for chandeliers that I made, custom designed for him, and he's going to sue me? I have heard of chutzpah. I have heard of gall. But this I never heard of."

"I'm truly sorry, Mr. Kellerman."

"You're sorry?"

"Yes."

"You're truly sorry?"

"Yes, sir."

"You want to hear sorry?"

"You're not going to do anything rash, are you, Mr. Kellerman?" asked Mickey.

"I wouldn't say 'rash.' No, not rash."

"Mr. Kellerman, please take my advice—"

"Advice? Are you sending me a bill for this advice?"

"No, sir."

"Good. Because I will now have to close up my business. And I couldn't afford your advice."

"Mr. Kellerman—"

"Don't 'Mr. Kellerman' me. You gave me enough Mr. Kellermans to last me ten lifetimes. Now, you know what is *touchas on tisch*?"

"No, sir."

"*Touchas on tisch* is Yiddish for 'put up or shut up.' For Mr. Crooked-as-a-politician, it means 'ass on the table.'"

"Mr. Kellerman, please, you'll have a heart attack."

"He owes me, Mr. Garagiola. I delivered those chandeliers six months ago. I custom made them to his designer's specs. Even if I could repossess them, who would I sell them to?"

I stood there helplessly. Kellerman would never believe it, but I was as powerless in this situation as he was.

"I'm begging you, do something. I staked my entire business on this job and he hasn't paid dime one on those chandeliers. Tell me something that's gonna remove my stomach from the ceiling. I walk around all day feeling like I have to vomit. That dirty, rotten, no-good, welching, four-flusher with his face on the cover of *Time* magazine. *Time* magazine should know how he's killing people. What kind of a person do you work for? I work eighteen hours a day trying to make a life, a business. I get a reputation. You want beautiful, custom-made crystal chandeliers like in the palace of Versailles? Call Kellerman. He'll make you chandeliers like the crowned heads of Europe danced under. No place else in America, in Europe, any place, will you get chandeliers like from Kellerman. Is this how he runs his business? Find an artist, ask for his life blood, drain every drop of it and then tell the artist to go fuck himself? He should die. With a case of incurable cancer, a heart attack, gallstones, kidney failure and a brain tumor. All together he should be stricken."

"Maybe we can get you on a list of preferred creditors," Mickey said lamely.

"Preferred creditors? Preferred creditors? What do I tell my grandchildren? That I was preferred by that lunatic? Look how my heart is beating through my jacket."

"That's the best I can do, Mr. Kellerman," said Mickey.

"Preferred creditors is not the best, Mr. Garagiola. Preferred creditors is the least worst."

"Did you try calling him, Mr. Kellerman?"

"Dozens of times. He's never in. He's in California, England, on his yacht, who knows where when I call him.

"He was around when he wanted the chandeliers quick. 'You'll stop everything, Kellerman, and make my chandeliers. You know why I'm coming to you, Mr. Kellerman? Because you are the greatest crystal craftsman in the modern world, Mr. Kellerman.' Butter wouldn't melt in his mouth how he sweet-talked me, promised me. And I swallowed it, hook, line and sinker. I stopped everything. I ran, I bought, I hired, and I created chandeliers like in heaven you'll see when you die. Mr. Garagiola, that man did me worse than dirt. He made as *mushkie* out of me.

"Do you know what's a *mushkie*? I'll tell you what's a *mushkie*. It's a broken man, that's what it is."

Mickey glanced at me and said, "I understand, Mr. Kellerman."

"No, you don't, Mr. Garagiola."

"I hear you, Mr. Kellerman."

"No, you do not. Or you wouldn't be able to live with yourself." He staggered out the door.

We walked down the hall to his office. He wasn't there.

"I just spoke with a Mr. Kellerman," Mickey said to The Mountebank's secretary. "Look, I don't know anything about chandeliers. But Mr. Kellerman is about to go out of his mind. And about to go bankrupt."

"There is nothing anyone can do. The boss made his decision."

"Do you remember Kellerman?" Mickey asked.

"Yes, he made chandeliers for us."

"What happened to them?"

"Why, he sold them to Bill Harrah for his new casino."

"Sold them? But he hasn't paid for them yet!"

She looked at us and shrugged. "He does it all the time."

The King's Ball

Liz and I were on vacation when I got the call. It was from you-know-who. He invited me to come down to his vast Florida spa on Cocoa Beach for lunch.

"Why didn't you warn me? How can I go to their home on three hours' notice?"

"He only just called me," I said. "Besides, it's informal."

"An informal lunch for twenty, Lester, informal? I've read about their informal lunches," she said, furiously poking through her suitcase. "I don't have time to shop."

"Shop? For what? First of all, you have enough clothes to last you three lifetimes. And shop for who? Do you know who's going to be at this thing?"

"A lot of very important people?"

"I suppose."

She modeled two dresses in a mirror. "How does this yellow look? It's old but expensive. I need to hem it."

I stretched out on the bed and watched my deliciously lithe wife scurry around looking for accessories. "Liz, you could show up in a flour sack and make this crowd look sick," I said.

We had just arrived for our vacation in Miami Beach when I received the call.

I was dumbfounded. He knew that I despised him and his grouchy wife. At least, I thought he knew. So what was the reason for inviting us?

Liz said, "I'll bet that all the other women will be wearing originals."

"They are as neurotic and insecure as the men are. Every time he farts they go into paroxysms. You should see them in the office. The phone rings and they run around like ants under attack. Yesterday one of the lawyers threw his back out when he thought he might be left off the guest list."

"You knew about this party yesterday, Lester? Yesterday? And you tell me about it three hours before we have to be there? Lester Colodny, you are a giant piece of doo-doo."

"I am not a giant anything. Maybe a little piece of turd. First of all, we weren't invited until this morning. So really, I think a giant piece of shit is a bit harsh."

"We were an afterthought?" she asked, looking up from her accessory box. "Not on the 'A' list, huh?"

"We are not even on their 'Z' list."

"So how did we get invited?"

"Who knows? He must have called and told the wife that some big muckymuck had dropped out and he probably said, 'Why don't we invite Lester and his wife?' Don't think for one second that she is all that thrilled with us sitting next to any of her pals. We are strictly subs sitting in for the first team."

"I can tell you really don't give a damn if we go or not," she said.

"I'd rather have a boil lanced."

"Who else is on the list? Did you see the list?"

"I peeked."

"I knew you would. Lester, you are so full of it."

"Being curious is not necessarily a sign of baloney."

She giggled and lay down on the bed next to me. She kissed my nose, my mouth, my neck and hugged me tightly. "Lester, my Lester. I love you, you yenta nosey-body. You wouldn't be caught dead with all those phonies but you found out fast enough who the phonies were who would be there."

"Only because it's important for me to know who he's opening his magnificent mouth to," I said. "It's my job to be on the alert for little bits of dirt and filth that will make my job easier to pay for your shopping and eating."

"Excuse me, sir, but what is your hand doing there?" she said. "Are you suggesting that we. . ."

"I certainly am," I whispered.

"What about the hem on the yellow dress?"

"The hell with the hem and the yellow dress. Do me," I whispered.

In the car, driving to Cocoa Beach, I said, "So why all of a sudden do you care about being at this lunch today? Since when did you decide the cognoscenti were worth rubbing shoulders with?"

She was polishing her nails. "No quick stops, please, driver," she said. "Actually, I have been dying to see their place. I hear it's an amazing estate. So what better way to see everything than being invited in the front door? This way I can go to their johns and explore their innermost sanctums."

"You wouldn't do that, would you?"

"I intend to discover their innermost design secrets. Whether their drapes are tacked or stitched. Whether the rugs are silk or wool and whether everything they own is fake or not."

"You are not only great in bed, you are a super snoop. God, how did I luck into such a wonder woman?"

"You must have been good in another life," she laughed as we pulled up to the gate at the estate. Uniformed attendants took the car and we proceeded to the main house.

We were both awestruck. It was incredible. Bedrooms, twenty-five of them, with bathrooms for each and every one. A seventy foot tower building, with a theater.

Oh, and in the back yard, a nine hole golf course.

When we entered the house, Liz gasped, "Lester, look at the size of those chandeliers."

"Remind me to tell you a story about chandeliers later."

"Tell me now."

"It's too good to waste. Later, tonight. In bed, after the lunch. I could get lucky twice in one day."

We stepped into the reception area of their vast quarters.

"Utterly unbelievable," Liz whispered.

At that moment, sweeping past several people, a bejeweled Mrs., in an Oscar de la Renta dress that must have cost a fortune, beamed at us.

"Informal," said Liz under her breath. "You idiot."

"He said informal," I replied lamely.

"So, hello Liz, it is so goot to see you again," she purred. "Vot a lovely outfit. And Lester, my love. I'm so glad you could come today. Come in, come in."

She took Liz's arm as if she were her oldest and dearest friend. "I vant you to meet everybody. They are so vonderful.

"My husband is the svitheart, don't you think, Liz? Who else vould come home vit not an emerald or a diamond tiara but tvin poodles for his vife. He is so romantic, my husband."

Liz glanced at me but I just shrugged.

It was a noisy affair, everyone talking at once. It may have been a luncheon for twenty, but if a bomb had hit the place, two-thirds of the nation's wealth would have been wiped out right then and there.

The Mrs. had a grip on Liz's arm and was shuttling her from one glitterati group to another.

Liz shot me a "what-do-I-do-now" look, but how was I going to tell her? She was on her own. I just wandered.

In the center of the room, I could see The Magic Raconteur holding court. He was being his most charming self and everybody was eating him up. He certainly had a way about him. The more his sycophants adored him, the brighter he shone.

A hand touched my shoulder and I turned to see a man in his early sixties sitting at the bar. He was very drunk. "Do you know I shaved thish company from bankruptshy?" he said to me. I looked around but there was no one else in hearing distance.

"Never mind how I did it," he said in response to a question I didn't ask. "I did it. And why did I do it?"

I shook my head.

"For shcumbags like you-know-who, that's who. That shit bag. That shon of a bitch. You know he craps on every shingle pershon who comes his way. In bishniss and in life." He looked at me blearily. "What do you do?"

"How do you know I do anything?" I said.

"Becaushe you're here. Anyone who'sh here does shomething for that lowlife. You poor schnook. I shuppose you jusht got sheduced by hish charm. I'm trying to help here, shave you from yourshelf, you dumb bashtard. Fine. Forget about it. Don't even know you. Why should I care?"

He got up off his barstool and tottered toward the double doors that led to the outer foyer. "Shayonara, adieu, and goodbye," he said.

He looked around, found two exquisite Egyptian vases that the lady of the house had placed just inside the doors, bent over, and threw up. In both of them.

Later that evening, on the way back to the hotel, I told Liz about the vomiter.

She looked at me knowingly. "Everyone, even falling down drunks are trying to warn you, Lester," she said.

I didn't respond.

"Alright, I'll change the subject. Guess what I overheard in one of the nine powder rooms?"

"Tell me."

"A certain 'vunderful, romantic' individual is keeping a certain young lady, with dark roots and large bosoms, in an apartment that he owns. And that certain young lady goes by the initial of L."

"No."

"Yes."

"How do you know this?" I asked.

"I overheard a certain gossip columnist who writes for *The New York Post*."

"And how did you know who this person was?"

"I looked in her wallet while she was taking a pee."

"Liz Colodny!" I said. "Looking in people's wallets."

"It was on the commode and it fell open. All I did was peek."

I said, "And that's why your man, the brilliant, incisive, perceptive writer of advertising is working day and night. To keep everyone busy and unaware of his shenanigans."

"Shenanigans? What an old fashioned word you use."

"What an old fashioned thing our leader does," I said.

The Other Barbara

I asked Liz, "Did you see the interview?"

"Did I see it? It was like watching one of those old movies where they throw the slaves in the arena to fight the lions. Putting that pea brain in the hands of Barbara should be reported to Amnesty International."

"He set it up himself," I added.

"I don't believe it," she said.

"I was there. In the office. He picked up the phone and called Barbara. 'She's coming out of the closet,' he says to Barbara. 'I want you to have the first exclusive interview with her, Barbara. Because you will treat her like a lady, Barbara.' That's exactly what he said. Then he says to me, 'I love that Barbara. Tough as fucking barbed wire. But a pro. A real pro.'"

"You know what that interview is going to cost him?" Liz asked me.

"With the divorce?"

"With the divorce, with everything. Mark my words, write it down, put it in an envelope and open it a year from now."

"Well, this admitting that they are openly jumping on one another will be the sorriest, dumbest, most destructive thing he has ever done. And let me tell you he has done some destroying in his short life. Only this time he has stepped on his own joint," I added.

"I don't agree. The world loves bastards. Look at all the movie stars running around having babies with each other. Affairs. Divorces."

"This will come back to haunt him. Mark my words. Bankers don't look at him like a movie star. To the banks, the man is collateral. Up to now he was worth a hundred and one cents on the dollar. Forty-four carat gold.

"Then," Liz opined, "this jerkwater ex-cheerleader goes on television and admits she's doing him and suddenly there's apples all over the street."

"The bankers get off the New Haven seven oh eight in Greenwich, Connecticut and the cute wife in the J. Hook outfit clucks to him how disgusting he is to his wife on national television. Because you can be sure the bankers' wives ate up every minute of Barbara's show plus what they gobble up every day in the *Enquirer* and Page Six in the *Post* and the ladies' magazines and all the gossip at the hairdressers and in the fitting rooms in Bendel's. And before you know it, all those white bread hypocrites who are banging their secretaries, are all sitting around some Rob Roys and doing what-ifs on our bond ratings.

"I tell you, the penchant our man has for media exposure will someday expose him and us, right in the toilet."

"Well, he doesn't know when to shut up," said Liz. "And now he's got this poodle babbling and licking her lips and saying dumb things on one of the most watched television shows. How fucking indiscreet can you be? Might as well buy time on the Super Bowl, drop your pants and show two billion people you've got holes in your underwear."

"My mother always inspected my underwear before I went out of the house. 'You never know,' she'd say. 'You could get hit by a truck.'"

You know, you'd think he had never had a mother. Brought up in an orphanage or something."

"Maybe he's a mutant. From another planet."

"The planet Schmuckola."

"Come to think of it, Lester, did you ever notice how much time we spend talking about him? What he said. What he did. Why he did it. What the papers wrote. What they said about him in the news. Jesus, you'd think our whole world revolved around him."

"Well, doesn't it?"

The King Calls

The phone rang.

I turned over and looked at the clock at my bedside.

"Who in the world would call at five thirty?" I said.

Liz turned over. "Who do you think?" she said.

I picked up the phone.

"Lester, I want to ask you something." It was him. The man who never slept. The genius who couldn't pronounce my name.

"Do you know what time it is?"

He ignored me. "Lester, do you think I could be president?" he asked.

"President of what?" I asked.

"The United States."

I couldn't believe it. Five thirty in the morning and he was asking me if I thought he could become the president. It was astonishing. President of the United States of America.

"You want to know if you could be elected president of the country?" I mumbled.

"Yes. I mean, who wouldn't vote for me?" he asked.

Who? Who? What was he thinking of? What was he talking about? And why was he asking me?

"I don't know," I said.

"There, you see? Lester, you think tremendous. You're the best. Tops. That's why I picked you to be my advisor. You have that kind of a mind. Ideas. Incisive. Fantastic. Outstanding."

It was nice to know that he thought all those things about me. But it was still five thirty-three. In the morning.

"I'm going to tell you something," he said. "I'm on my way to Maine now, to put my foot in the ocean."

"I think you mean your toe," I corrected him. "In the water."

"Yeah, yeah, my toe."

I said, "But you'll need a lot of people to vote for you."

"Lester, anybody who's anybody knows who I am."

"But will they think of you as their president? There are a lot of nobodies who have the same vote as anybodies. And when it comes to voting, there's sometimes more nobodies than anybodies." There. Take that, I harrumphed under my breath.

"What?" said Liz.

"Be quiet," I said, "I'm talking to the next President of the United States."

"What did you say?" he asked.

I thought quickly, then I said, off the top of my insane mind, "Maybe you ought to think about running as a Democrat."

There was a long silence. He was thinking. Then he said, softly, "Why would I run as a Democrat? I'm a billionaire."

Without missing a beat, I said, "Well, Rockefeller should have run as a Democrat. If he had, he'd still be president."

Another long silence. Then, "Rockefeller is dead."

I said, "If he were a Democrat he'd still be alive." If that doesn't do it, nothing will. I held my breath.

He said, "If Rockefeller had run as a Democrat he'd still be alive? What the fuck are you talking about? Besides, what do you know about running for president?"

Just then I heard the sound of helicopter engines and I realized that he was at the heliport. I knew that anything I could have said that would have been understood would also have been drowned out. So I mumbled.

"What?" he yelled.

I mumbled something else incoherently.

He slammed the receiver down. Apparently, the rotors had revved and he was off to Maine to put his foot in the ocean.

My wife turned over and sat up.

"What in hell was that all about?" she asked.

"You won't believe what just happened."

"I can imagine."

"He asked me, you're not going to believe this, if I thought he could be president."

"So? What else is new? And I heard what you said."

"What else did you expect me to say?"

She said. "I hope, Mr. Kiss Ass, when they find your dead body, your lips are not attached to his backside."

I also heard about it later on:

"Why does walking away from a bad situation make you a bad guy? When you first started, you told me you did what you do for him because you enjoyed doing it. But now you're acting like the megalomaniac that he is. What makes you think you can get away with that kind of behavior? Do you think you can really influence what's going on?"

"I don't know."

"Lester, you don't even know how unimportant you really are in this bad mini-series you're living. You think you can control the behavior of the principal player?"

"No. I'm not that stupid," I said.

"You're sailing a toy sailboat in a typhoon. Listen to me, Lester, please. You are a writer trying to make up a script while you're watching the movie."

"I can't leave now," I protested.

"Why not?" she said. "Give me one example, one iota of a reason for hanging on to this stinking ship. I didn't say sinking. I said stinking. Listen to me. When the going gets too tough even the tough get out. There is a definite difference between bravery and martyrdom.

"What I can't fathom is your determination, in the face of overwhelming odds, for such an unworthy, unrewarding cause. You're not a fool. You hate fools. You detest folly. And yet, for all these months you've driven the recon jeep ahead of this general's army. You've cleared land mines, blown snipers away, thrown your body on live hand grenades.

"You know—this Christmas I'm going to buy you a do-it-yourself crucifixion kit. 'Put nail A into right hand.' It's too painful to watch. What's the prize? What do you win if you win?"

I said meekly, "The prize, I suppose is. . .not losing."

"All right, pal. Not losing? Guess what his eminence pulled today?"

"What?"

"There's a good chance that he's going into bankruptcy."

"Huh?"

"That's right. In Atlantic City. I can't believe I'm telling you," she said.

"Where did you hear that?"

"On the radio."

"You heard it on the news and I don't know a thing about it?" I said.

"Lester, you have your nose so far up his rear end that you can't hear anything."

"Do you think that he's up to something? Something we ordinary mortals don't have an inkling about?"

"Lester, he is a genius. You want to know why? Because he thinks of doing things that we would never dream of doing. Unto other people. Ruthlessly and relentlessly."

I said, "I know, I know whatever he does isn't exactly kosher."

"No, it isn't."

"So?"

"So?"

"Yes, what do you suggest I do?" I asked plaintively.

"I don't suggest anything. It's your life."

"But you're my wife," I said. "Remember? In sickness and in health. And stuff like that."

"What do you want?"

"Tell me. What should I do?" I finally said.

"Lester, you are a grown man. Fully in control of your own choices and decisions. You know what to do. Do it."

Hail Mary

We were sitting in a box on the fifty yard line and The Boss was haranguing me.

"This is an important game, Lester. Lotsa big money involved here. Sixty-five thousand people here in this stadium. Maybe two billion watching on television. And what does the cameras focus on? Me."

"Got it," I said. "And you don't want them to see you with a knockout blonde with long hair, long legs, and great tits hanging all over you. They get to see you with me."

"Sometimes you're not so dumb, Lester. That's what counts—the big picture. That's why I'm where I am in this world. Because I always look for the big picture. Make sure I'm on top, looking down."Hey," he said, switching gears, "you ever get fucked in a limo, Lester?"

"All the time, sometimes two and three times a day."

"Really?"

"By you," I said. It went right over his head.

"What do you think about my girl?" he asked.

"I don't want to think about anything but what a game this is gonna be."

"She's very smart."

"Let's go, Jets," I yelled.

"I'm thinking maybe we make her the president of one of our casinos in Atlantic City."

I turned to him. "You. . .are putting me on. Tell me this is your twisted way of making a joke," I said.

"I don't joke about money, Lester."

"What the fuck does a girl like that know about the gambling business?"

"She told me she was a head cocktail waitress in Reno. Worked for Bill Harrah."

"She told you she was a head cocktail waitress? And you're going to make her the president of a billion dollar hotel and casino? Where is your brain, sir? Has she sucked it out of you?"

"I don't know what you're talking about," he said.

"Dee-fence, dee-fence," I chanted along with the sixty-five thousand other screaming fans.

"I think maybe you could be taking a little on the side," he shouted.

"I know you're getting something on the side," I said. "And when are you going to learn that there are some people in the world who do not have larceny in their souls?" I was getting very, very tired of his bullshit.

"Name six," he shouted over the roars of the crowd.

"Mother Teresa, for one," I yelled.

"Maybe," he bellowed.

"Maybe? Mother Teresa? You are sick. Now please. Let me watch these guys kick some ass."

In the middle of the second quarter he yelled, "Let's get out of here. I want to beat the crowd."

"Jesus Christ," I growled. "You drag me away from my wife, who I haven't said hello to for about six months because I'm so busy with your business, to be your fake date at this game and then you want to leave before half time to beat the crowd? If you don't mind, I want to see the rest of this game."

"I need you," he said in my ear. "If you're with us she will at least be civil. Well, half civil. She won't rant and rave. And I have a bad headache about your fucking fees and if you're not with me at the apartment and she starts breaking my balls, I'm liable to cut your fee right in half. I've been going over your bills, Lester. You're ripping me off. You are, you know."

"First of all, you've threatened to cut my fee in half at least thirty times this year. So by now I should be working for about a dime an hour. Second of all, I am not going to defend my fees. Pay the frigging bills or get somebody else."

A good friend of mine, who was also invited to watch the game, chose to sit in the TV truck where he had a bird's eye view of the game and the choice visual of every camera angle. The next time I saw him he told me the director was going wild, shouting into his headset.

"Camera six, camera eight. Somebody gimme a tight shot on that lunatic in box twelve. Yeah. It's him."

"Looks like he's lost his fucking mind. Look at him, waving his hands, yelling at the guy next to him."

"Who cares about the game? We'll get back to it. This is great television."

"Good, camera six, good. Yeah. Yeah. Okay. Now go in close. Closer. Get as tight as you can. Let's see what the other guy's saying."

"'Fuck you? Don't give me that shit?' Oh, camera six, I will kiss your ass for this. Okay, at the end of the next commercial break we replay it. The audience can read his lips for themselves."

"If we don't have the biggest rating in the history of sports, I will kiss Roone Arledge's ass on *Good Morning America*."

"Now, let's get back to the game."

"You know," the director said, turning to smile at my friend, "It's the little things in life that make this all worthwhile."

That night I finally told Liz what had happened to Mr. Kellerman. She said, "Doesn't your skin begin to crawl?"

I said, "His actions do have a disturbing quality about them."

"Lester, a disturbing quality?"

"It's big business, high finance. That is how that world functions. And always has."

"Lester."

"I know. They have a distinct aroma about them."

"They stink."

"You might say that."

"They're awful."

"You might say that, too."

"And you're not. Or at least you never used to be. Lester, you have to get out of there. Now."

"I have a certain monetary obligation that I'm forced to consider," I said.

"You're selling your soul, Lester. You point the finger at him and say, 'I'm just following orders.' Well, this isn't the military and you do have a choice."

I didn't say anything.

"You don't realize what has happened to you, do you? What you've become over the last seven years."

I refused to respond.

"Lester, it's time. Actually, it's way past time. And you know it."

I looked away.

"Lester, if you don't quit—"

"What?" I demanded.

"If you don't, I'm quitting you."

"You wouldn't."

"Oh yes, I would."

"You can't be serious. Why would you?"

"Because you are changing. In fact, you have changed."

"Into what?"

There was a very long pause.

"Into a sleaze bag."

"A sleaze bag? That is a very indelicate term, my love," I said.

"And you have become a very indelicate person," Liz said.

She looked at me pointedly, then moved across the room to the closet and pulled out a suitcase.

"Where are you going?" I asked (my heart in my shoes).

"On a trip."

"To where?"

There was no response. Just the sounds of drawers being slammed open and clothing being thrown into the case.

I watched her as she finished her packing. Then she put on her coat and said, "I'll send for the rest of my things."

"You're not serious, Liz, come on—"

She stopped at the bedroom door and looked searchingly at me. There was a long, long silence.

"What ever happened to Lester Colodny?" she said and left.

I was speechless. I walked around the empty apartment and said aloud, "Liz?"

But there was no answer. No Liz.

I ran to the elevator but it had gone down.

Dashing down the eleven flights of stairs, I ran out into the street. She was getting into a cab.

"Liz," I shouted. "Please wait. Where are you going?"

She turned around. "Where?" she said quietly. "Where I can breathe again." The cab pulled away.

I wandered around the apartment, saying her name. I knew in the deepest part of my soul that Liz was right. What had I become but a damned fool who had forsaken a lifetime of dreams, aspirations and hopes. For what?

For money. It was true. Everything he asked me or told me to do, wanted me to do, encouraged me to do, I did, because he paid me a whole lot of money. I was overwhelmed by a miasma, a bog of shame.

I looked at my face in the bathroom mirror. What stared back at me made me sick.

I ran to the phone and started to dial. On the fourth ring, I got lucky.

"Yes?"

"Liz, you were so right," I blurted out. "You are so damned right. I don't know what came over me."

She said, "I know. It was all green but it smelled like you know what."

"Liz," I begged. "Liz, I'm resigning. I'm getting out."

"He'll sue you."

"Let him."

"He'll blackball you," she said. "Spread stories of perversion, incompetence, even embezzlement."

"Who cares? It'll be the dream of my life being zapped in the press by the world's most awful person. I could be an overnight sensation. A superstar. I might even get an offer to write a book. But I don't care. I don't care about anything. I want my Liz back, do you hear?"

"You mean it?"

"Liz. Please. I'll be waiting at the airport. Just tell me what plane you'll be on and I'll be there. I love you, Liz. Where are you?"

She said, "If you mean it—"

"I've never meant anything more in my life, Liz. Never," I pleaded. "Where are you?"

"Downstairs, in the lobby."

After All That

Before I could quit, he fired me.

When I got to the office the next morning, ready to tell him that I was leaving, Mickey Garagiola came into my office, shut my door behind him, and told me that The Man was furious with me.

"Why?" I asked.

"Because he pays you too much money."

"You're kidding me. He's the one who keeps giving me raises. I never asked for an extra dime."

"He said that you made too much money and that he's firing you."

"What does he want me to do? Take back my adjectives?"

I feigned being indignant. "I have a contract," I said. "In fact, I have three contracts. I'll sue him." (The elephant and the mouse!)

"He said I should sue you."

Now this was a dance I knew the steps to. "What will he sue me for?"

"He doesn't need anything to sue you for. He can just hang your ass-ets up in court for years, decades."

"I see," I said. "And you said?"

"I said okay, I'll sue him."

"And are you suing me?"

"Nah. If I can get you forty cents on the dollar for the rest of your contracts will you take it?"

I couldn't believe it. Here I was, ready to walk out with nothing and Garagiola was offering me forty cents on the dollar. A quitting bonus.

I didn't want to give in too quickly so I said, "Let me think about it."

He said, "Lester, this has to be a take it or leave it. Now."

I said quickly, "I'll take it."

He pulled a check out of his pocket and handed it to me. It was made out to Lester Colodny, Inc. And it equaled forty cents on the dollar for the rest of what was due me.

I smiled at him. "You did this for me?"

He replied, "If he knew I was giving you any settlement he would rip my balls off. He can't stand anyone surviving after he's put them on his hit list."

I said, "Thank you, Mr. G."

"Good luck, kiddo," he answered.

I took the check and went across the street to the bank and cashed it. What luck. What dumb, beautiful luck.

I called Liz. "Guess what?" I yelled.

"Tell me," she said.

"We're going on a trip. To Paris, London, Rome and all points east."

After all that, I tried my hand at this and that. An ad for an acne cure here, a commercial for a toilet bowl cleaner there, but nothing had the same kick that I had had through the years.

I was wiped out.

I retired.

Kim and Kathy got married. Mace opened a restaurant, Liz' oldest son Kevin and her daughter Lisa married, and her middle son, Michael, went out west to seek his fortune.

We eventually had twelve grandchildren and a dog named Oscar. As I looked back over the years, I realized that I had had one hell of a run.

Win some, lose some.

But it was a great ride while it lasted.

Susan Heller was interviewed by Nikki Andrews,
the editor of *A Funny Thing Happened…*

NA: So, what was this experience like?

SH: What? Working with Lester? Utterly insane. Magnificent. Splendiferous. Favorite project ever. I know you think I have to say that, and he did slip me five bucks. But in the Entertainment Dictionary under *Character* it says, "You have to ask? What, you don't know Lester Colodny?"

NA: Seriously, you're a writer, producer and director yourself. I know you write scripts, articles, stories, you've co-authored historical biographies and done a lot of ghost writing as well. So how…

SH: (Interrupting rather rudely) *How* is not even the right question. Lester is the human equivalent of spontaneous combustion. This man has funny DNA. Everywhere he goes, funny stuff happens. I had a blast.

NA: Um, excuse me but this is supposed to be a bio of you and…

SH: And for these purposes, my take on him is more revelatory than a list of credits about me. I told him that writing about his life was way more fun than living mine. I tend to stay under the radar – you won't find me on FaceBook or Twitter. Lester is larger than life. In addition to the funny, there is the sensitive and courageous side of all comedians. Make no mistake, Lester is above all, a story-teller, a comedian. I learned a tremendous amount from him.

Plus, his opinions are always, always on the money.

NA: (Waving a typewritten page in her hand) Are you referring to this letter he wrote to the publisher, James Maynard?

SH: I really couldn't say. That would be most immodest of me. But you can print an excerpt if you'd like.

NA: (Rolling her eyes skyward) Here it is.

"I was introduced to Ms. Susan Heller. After some discussion, we agreed that she would help with the manuscript. I must admit I was skeptical.

Since that time many months ago, she has become an indispensable partner, writing, rewriting, adding, subtracting. The result is this new manuscript…which would not, and could not, have been accomplished without Ms. Heller's unique talent.

Her input, her revisions, her writing and admonitions for me to stay true to the truth has made it what it is. This book is a true collaboration. And I hope the reader will enjoy it as much as we did in producing it."

Lester Colodny.

SH: Me too.